Voyage of the Yellow Submarine

A multi-voice chronicle of life in a commune

By
Tuna Cole, Pip Cole, and Crew

Crew members in this collective narrative include Nepal T Blalock; Joe, Tammy, and Gary Brittain; Vernette Christensen; James Livingston; John Richey; Jerry Rust; Gail Sanford; Pollo Smith; and Quarrel Stockton—in addition to Tuna and Pip Cole.

One cover concept and Eugene skyline photograph by Tuna Cole
The other cover concept and art by Pip Cole
Graphic design by Lindsey Streitz
Photographs throughout by Tom Emmens, unless otherwise noted
Line Drawings by Linda Brittain Flanagan.

Voyage of the Yellow Submarine
A multi-voice chronicle of life in a commune
Tuna Cole, Pip Cole, and Crew
Copyright 2012

ISBN: 978-0-9855702-0-0

Keywords: commune, hippies, Vietnam War, counterculture, the Resistance, draft resistance, 60s rock 'n' roll, psychedelics, ethnography, New Age spirituality

First Printing: May 2012

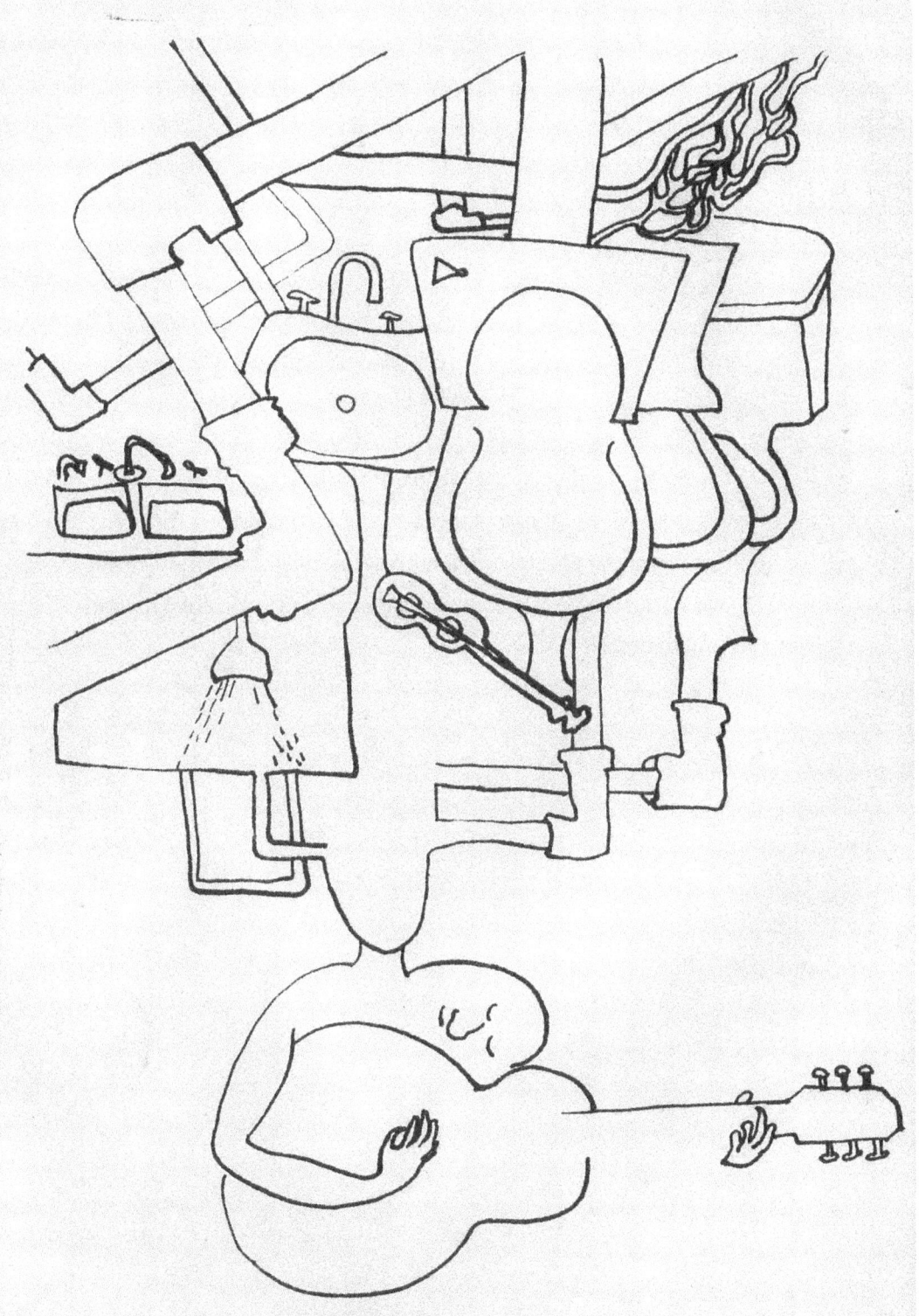

Dedication

Here's to us, aging curmudgeons, mostly—a tragicomedy of geriatric irascibility—for holding together and seeing this project through.

And here's to the next generation—born-again hippies, or far from it. We wish for you wisdom and patience and luck. Like as not, you're going to need them.

Foreword

The idea of writing out this story has been kicking around for decades. Of course those who expressed interest dithered. We moved around. We had families, occupations, and hobbies that made up the bulk of our lives. However, many of us kept in touch, fellow veterans as we were, and so the notion of a group effort at telling the story of our communal experience was kept raw and contused, rather than "nurtured," exactly—more like a burr down your collar, or a small pebble in your shoe, than a radiant beacon of inspiration.

By about three years ago, it began to dawn on a core of us yet-compos mentis communard vets that our ranks were thinning out at an alarming rate. We'd better get crackin' if we had any hope of actually compiling anything like a multiple narrative. Fortunately thirteen people among that shrinking circle of former participant/members and our associates were willing to offer their perspectives on that experience from so long ago. Chanren Ragman, Anita Larsen, Pollo Smith, Gale Sanders, Elvis Boinker, John Richey, Jerry Ferrox, Quarrel Stockton, James Livingston, Geary, Jay, and Candy Button, and yours truly, Yowell Mebsanuri, have all made contributions. Unless otherwise indicated, the text in this section was written by Yowell Mebsanuri. Most of the other contributors share space with brother Chanren's observations through the Portal of the Antipodes, the down-under cover.

Names have been changed for most participants, perhaps out of an excess of caution to protect the sensitivities of our contemporaries, some of whom may not look forward to reliving—let alone publicizing—those good ol' days, having managed to put so many miles between them and the subject at hand.

A close reading among the various accounts will yield

anomalies. We considered trying to reconcile these discrepancies, but in the end, opted to permit each offering as a unique, valid statement in its own right. People remember what they remember.

A good deal of cognitive effort has gone into characterizing this work. What manner of beast is it? A collective memoir? A case-study, an ex-urban ethnographic graduate-level thesis in Anthropology? A drug-induced hallucination/acid flashback? Gasp…Fiction? It is my considered belief that these accounts represent our recollections—as best we can recall—to be sure, tarted up/teased out a bit here and there, in the manner of a burlesque, in an attempt at drawing the contrast between mainstream America and the breakaway counterculture experience we were very much a part of ca late 1960s. At the same time, we weren't above chumming the literary waters in hopes of stimulating some readership with a few lubricious details.

Perhaps we should celebrate any ability to re-imagine events from so many decades ago. Besides, who's to say precisely how events transpired forty-plus years after the experience? Yowie actually wrote up some notes on his experience of the Yellow Submarine soon after jumping ship in late 1970, the basis for many of these episodes. But I'm getting ahead of myself.

A word needs to be said about voice. The reader may be fidgeting in vague unease as to who is doing the presenting here. Contributors to this over-all compendium are entitled to wear different hats, according to the roles they are willing to assume in the narrative and meta-narrative. For example, a person could be describing an event s/he was participant to. It would be appropriate for such an account to be in first person, presumably past tense.

This same person could be introducing the idea of the book to a curious and tight-fisted audience—a very different role, you must admit—and have every right to be concerned that his/her lexical prestidigitation might not be enticing enough to "sell" the book in a necessarily brief passage of words (after all, if it's about the story, a preview, it is not the story itself). If that were the case, s/he might bait that hook with a range of seductions and allures: wild and incongruous imagery, strangely juxtaposed narrative styles, anything to get the curious reader to take a bite.

Third person presentation—to lend an air of formality and objectivity—is likely to be one of the machinations, tricks, if you insist, used to accomplish the hooked fish, er, eager reader. I sometimes portray myself in the third person in the narrative. Various episodes from so long ago take on aspects of another person/another life from the perspective of current affairs. It has been easier to describe those events by characterizing myself as other.

Finally, some contributors to this group recollection want it made explicit that one's contribution in no way implies s/he condones or approves comments or points of view expressed by other contributors. Each of us owns his/her individual contribution, with consanguinity thereafter on a case-by-case basis.

There's an old chestnut that states, If you can recollect the '60s you weren't there; if you were really "there" you can't remember much of anything. Suggesting, one too many surges in the ol' brain circuitry. That double-fist-sized mass of putty cradled in your skull suffered sensory overload somewhere along the way. Blown to smithereens by sex, drugs and rocknroll. This Voyage is a mitigation of that adage.

Chill out, bro; here's how it went down…

Voyage of the Yellow Submarine

*If my words did glow with the glow of sunshine
And my tunes were played on the harp unstrung,
Would you hear my voice come through the music,
Would you hold it near as it were your own?*

*It's a hand-me-down, the thoughts are broken,
Perhaps they are better left unsung.
I don't know, don't really care,
Let there be songs to fill the air.*

*Ripple in still water
When there is no pebble tossed,
Nor wind to blow*

*Reach out your hand if your cup be empty,
If your cup is full, may it be again
Let it be known there is a fountain
That was not made by the hands of man.*

*There is a road, no simple highway,
Between the dawn and the dark of night,
And if you go, no one may follow,
That path is for your steps alone.*

*Ripple in still water
When there is no pebble tossed
No wind to blow*

*You who choose to lead must follow
But if you fall you fall alone,
If you should stand, then who's to guide you?
If I knew the way, I would take you home...*

Ripple, The Grateful Dead

Contents

Guided by the North Star

Social Landmarks	1
Every One of Us…Introduction to Yowell Mebsanuri	5
Genesis	5
A Different Planet	10
A Yellow Submarine Précis	12
Finances	14
Dichotomies	17
The Digs	28
Food and All That Pertains	33
Anita's Tale (Pt. 1)	38
Hendrix Park	45
The Yellow Sub Cottage Industry	49
The Pull to Pair	52
The Reconnaissance/Recruitment Trip	56
William Blake Made Manifest in Jim Morrison	64
The US Census Bureau Encounters the Yellow Submarine	66
Confirming/Debunking Myths	68
The New World	71
Hair	75
The Three Stooges Encounter Three Graces	77
The Dispossession of Earthly goods	79
Pets	80
The Yellow Sub Repels Grosse Pointe Assault	83
Fire!	87

"Rivendale"	90
The Golden Age of Chemistry	92
Disclaimer	95
The Story of Elvis Boinker	96
The Swinging Pendulum	98
Notes of Rage	107
The Saga of the Mamarone	109
Rock and Roll	111
When the Music's Over…	118
Conclusions	120
Anita's Tale (Pt. 2)	122
Epilogue	129
The Meta-Narrative: The Process of Writing this Book	133
Acknowledgements	138

from l. Wayne, Jeffrey, James & May, Yowie, Pollo, Gagutz, Doris, Quarrel, Malcolm, Chanren, Anita, & Mudra. Autumn '68.

Social Landmarks

11/22/63: JFK assassinated, Vice President Lyndon Baines Johnson becomes President

7/2/64: Johnson signs the Civil Rights Act, prohibiting discrimination in housing, jobs, & other public places; permits integration in schools

8/7/64: Congress passes Gulf of Tonkin Resolution granting LBJ authority to wage "conventional" war on North Vietnam without Congressional War Declaration; Oregon Senator Wayne Morse is one of only two Senators to vote against surrendering this constitutionally mandated authority

8/6/65: Johnson signs the Voting Rights Act, banning racial discrimination in states' registration of voters

12/31/65: 184,000 American troops in Vietnam, 1863 fatalities that year

6/20/66: Rolling Stones release Aftermath

8/8/66: Beatles release Revlover

12/31/66: 389,000 American troops in Vietnam, 6143 fatalities that year

1/7/67: The Doors release their self-titled album

2/?/67: The Jefferson Airplane releases Surrealistic Pillow

6/2/67: Beatles release Sgt. Pepper's Lonely Heart's Club Band

8/23/67: Jimmy Hendrix releases Are You Experienced

12/31/67: 487,000 American troops in Vietnam, 11,153 fatalities that year

4/4/68: Martin Luther King Jr. assassinated

6/5/68: Robert Kennedy Assassinated

8/12/68: Big Brother & the Holding Company (Janis Joplin) releases Cheap Thrills, the most popular album of the year with +/- million albums sold

11/5/68: Richard Nixon elected President with only 43.4 %, compared to Humphrey's 42.7 %, of votes—3rd party candidate George Wallace taking the remainder

11/25/68: Beatles release White Album

12/6/68: Rolling Stones release Beggar's Banquet

12/31/68: 535,000 American troops in Vietnam, 16,592 fatalities that year

1/12/69: Led Zeppelin releases its first, self-titled album

1/13/69: Beatles release Yellow Submarine

7/14/69: Release date for immensely successful counter-culture movie "Easy Rider"

7/29/69: Neil Armstrong, "Buzz" Aldrin become first men on the moon

10/1/69: Beatles release Abbey Road

11/15/69: Crowds estimated at 500,000 marched in Washington DC and San Francisco to protest the continuing Vietnam War—several Yellow Submarine members participated in San Francisco

12/5/69: Rolling Stones release Let It Bleed

12/31/69: 475,000 American troops in Vietnam, 11,616 fatalities that year

5/1/70: National Guardsmen shoot/kill four students at antiwar protest, Kent State University, Ohio

4/10/70: Paul McCartney publicly announces breakup of Beatles (John Lennon had announced privately in September '69)

5/18/70: Beatles release Let It Be

12/?/70: Eric Clapton et al. release Derek & the Dominos

7/1/71: 26th Amendment to the Constitution ratified, lowering voting age from 21 to 18

8/14/71: The Who release Who's Next

4/30/74: Final evacuation day of American personnel from Vietnam. Over 56,000 American fatalities, two million Vietnamese fatalities (est.). Seven million tons of bombs had been dropped—"more than twice the total bombs dropped on Europe and Asia in World War II" (Howard Zinn, People's History of the US). Between 1964~'75 some 3.5 million men served in the Vietnam theater, of whom 2,215,000 had been conscripted

Every one of us is all we need...
　　　　　　　　　　　　　　　　Yellow Submarine, The Beatles

Herein the disparate, desperate ravings of Yowell Mebsanuri (aka Yowie), the assumed name of a crewmember and co-participant/co-conspirator of the Yellow Submarine, a suburban commune he helped found, name, and navigate. For Yowie, this was a shared experience, a part of him, like a scar, however far from that house or those people the currents may take him.

<u>Genesis</u>

In the beginning were Pollo and his son Gagutz in situ, Eugene, Oregon. Then came Chanren and Anita, who begat Karisma, our waif. Together they rented this slightly dingy, post-war, three-story house in a terrific setting, August 1968. Number Six in somesort of cosmic seniority, I got to Eugene one week later, after 36 hours of straight hitching from Flagstaff, a hot, grueling, but uneventful trip except for getting busted for hitch-hiking on the freeway in the middle of the night in Fresno.

It is ironic that within the month of our communal launch, the Democratic National Convention was underway in Chicago, choosing the party candidate, Hubert Humphrey, to lose against Nixon in November. The nation watched in stunned fascination the surreal contrast between the cheery, upbeat, party atmosphere among the delegates inside the convention hall, while outside, literally within shouting distance, the city displayed its vicious and wantonly violent side in quelling the antiwar demonstrations, in what came to be known as the Days of Rage. This game-changing event for confrontational protest mostly passed us by; we didn't own a TV, didn't subscribe to the paper, and rarely listened to the radio. We were intent on creating a different history...

You could argue, of course, that the beginning of the beginning came with the idea, that initial cognitive impulse, occurring ineluctably before the willed act. Said kernel was promulgated by Quarrel Stockton in a group mailing in early spring of 1967. Simply stated, it was the desire to live in somesort of unspecified communal arrangement, and so he raised the issue for general consideration. The idea, or something like it, must have been close to our consciousness, otherwise how to account for the ease with which so many of us were induced to follow our fantasies?

While the notion simmered, several of us investigated various locations around central and southern Arizona in Chanren and Anita's VW bus. We spent some time prowling around Jerome and Bisbee; the former, never a complete "ghost town," but having discovered the entrepreneurial possibilities of its quaint status, was on the cusp of developing various enticements (B&Bs, local schlock/curio shops, restaurants) to fleece the visitors. Bisbee, a much bigger and more recently-active mining town, wasn't a ghost town by a long shot, but was in the long slide. Block after block of decaying buildings with vistas of despoiled landscape. Both towns offered extensive, enclosed, private spaces on the cheap—in which to perpetuate our personal separateness? Neither offered anything external, natural, to cultivate, to develop a relationship with. Can you have a relationship with desolation?

Pollo had sought out Eugene inasmuch as the U of O extracted no out-of-state tuition fees to grad students. He was there as a fine arts grad at no more expense than, say, ASU would have tapped him for. By contrast to most of his life in Tucson, Eugene must have seemed like a kind of paradise, a hippie faeryland. In short order, he let it be known that in our search for a benign environment for somesort of communal living arrangement, we could do a lot worse than the Emerald Empire. Several of us even made an exploratory probe to check out the vibe, again in Chanren 'n' Nita's VW van that early-summer of '68, and found the Eugene setting paradisiacal, indeed.

Ripe for colonization.

There's something happening here, what it is ain't exactly clear
There's a man with a gun over there, telling me I got to beware...
Battle lines being drawn, nobody's right if everybody's wrong
Young people speaking their mind, gettin' so much resistance from behind
I think it's time we stop, children, what's that sound?
Everybody look what's going down

For what it's worth, Buffalo Springfield

So we were going to be a commune… One year after that first foray, we were becoming a commune, whatever that was. The first thing that was evident about taking on the communal identity was it was a farce. We had used the word, commune, to speak of how we intended to live together. But the word didn't contain any clues as to how that would happen. A farce, a little charade we were willing to perform—for others' benefit, or ourselves? Merely a game, each person acting out his/her role. Wait! You don't play games with people's lives.

Really? Too often the game, the role, the performance, comes to take up too much of the meaningful interactive aspects of life; it remains, for better or worse, a part of socialization. Some games are quite serious, others are light-hearted and fun, and still worth "playing." Furthermore, there are games within games: The politeness gestures, conversational turn-taking, the "rules" we buy into at all levels in order to be admitted as a player. Observe these few conventions and we'll co-municate; otherwise stay out there on your own, if you prefer. Boarding house, or commune, or crash pad, it's just a question of what kind/how much of the image you adopt.

And therein lay a secret: the more you believe, and espouse, and act out an identity the more it becomes-you-become-it. For better or worse. We are what we think/believe we are, what we <u>practice</u>... (sounds like something straight out of the mouth of a stone freak). In any event, enough of the early group, the nexus—via a 36-hour-non-stop-"marathon"-stay-in-the-present-talk-it-out-therapy session—thought it important to codify us, in the process of giving ourselves a handle on the physical manifestation of who/what we were.

What would we call ourselves, then? We needed to distinguish ourselves from the five or six area communes we'd heard of. We needed a moniker. I remember the occasion as if it were a mere 40 years ago: We'd gathered several gunnysacks full of walnuts as part of our gleaning campaign. After drying them and removing the husks (a nasty job!), we'd sit in a big circle around a pile of walnuts and crack them to separate the meat from the shells, destined for our earliest attempts at the revolutionary cereal, granola (more on that later). This was a painstaking, slow process—arguably, the most labor-intensive project we ever tried, at perhaps two person/hours per pound of shelled walnuts—and copious amounts of Doña Maria Juana were considered efficacious. Even so, such occasions didn't occur often; harvesting enough walnut meat by hand for what grew to be a 50~60 lb-per-day commercial breakfast cereal operation would have been madness.

Nevertheless, on one such event, the Yellow Submarine was tossed in the ring for consideration as our communal name. The house was a dull babyshit-off-yellow, no getting around it. And while I was a Stones man myself—the Dirty Beatles!—it was hard to deny that the Fab Four, with the recent release of their White Album, had demonstrated, again—as with everything since Sgt. Pepper's Lonely Hearts' Club Band—they could do no wrong.

As "mature" Beatles' songs go, The Yellow Submarine was a lightweight, with some clever gimmicks and a phrase or two that were metaphorically apt. I don't recall the name ever being explicitly, formally voted upon or otherwise ratified, but then, voting wasn't really our style anyway. As a hook, the name wasn't particularly euphonious. Coming in at five syllables, it didn't exactly roll off the tongue mellifluously. Nevertheless, within a short amount of time, the name had settled in and become our recognized mantle.

*****

Continuing the chronology of Yellow Submarine crew members, next came James Livingston, testing the waters, followed a couple of weeks later by wife May and Jeffrey, their son, a little younger than Gagutz. Then Wayne Amos, our geriatric, sometime writer. And Malcolm and Mudra, fellow war resisters from Tucson, and their two big malamute/huskies. Along in here I got hired as a seasonal at the local "Diamond A" Cannery where I met Tom Emmens. This PhD-candidate dropout from the U of O was so taken by the sprouting of a suburban commune in his own town, that he hung around a lot, and became the house photographer—so much so that early on some people thought he was a not-so-undercover narc. He responded by giving us a closet full of canned goods, from three different styles/preparations of corn (Tumor's advice: Never eat "cream-style" corn), to green beans, peas, beets, carrots, pears, plums, peaches, blackberries and several other comestibles. His generosity toward our larder was so helpful and appreciated that he was more or less adopted by acclamation, becoming a kind of "non-resident member" thereafter.

Then came a local maiden, Marta, she of the fiery-red hair, all by the end of nineteen sixty-eight.

A Different Planet

It's interesting to see the psychic changes, the climatological adjustments we Arizona folks (the first ten or eleven Submariners without exception, all Arizona invaders) went through as the seasons changed. To the unfortunate reader who has thus far been deprived of up-close-and-personal "quality time" in Arizona over, say, a continuous year of residence: It is a desert. Annual precip in Phoenix, "Valley of the Sun," central Arizona, is just over 8.5 inches. In a good year. Most of spring, all of summer, and most of fall are stifling and oppressive. Without the ability, thanks to technology, to live inside containers of controlled temperature and humidity, life would be unendurable to all but the Australian Aborigines in the summertime, and even they wouldn't like it. The only hope of surviving 2/3 of every year is to turn inward to sanctuaries of evaporative coolers (in the days of my childhood), nowadays refrigeration. Or scurrying to and from such havens. A sliver of fall and early spring, and the whole of winter, by contrast, were sunny, for the most part; warm during the days and outwardly inviting. It would take somesort of Arctic scenario to provide a greater contrast to the Willamette Valley than southern Arizona.

Skinner's Mudhole, the Emerald Empire, the city well-born, drinks up or sheds over 50 inches—over four feet!—of precipitation per annum, mostly in winter, with significant contributions in fall and spring. Sometimes, a fair amount comes to us in summer (God help us!). Six times the amount of rainfall we desert dwellers were used to makes a conspicuous difference to the landscape, let me tell you. This moisture blows straight off the largest body of water in the world, the Pacific Ocean—read wet, lush, diverse, abundant photosynthetic growth. What hasn't been cut is a rainforest, a temperate rainforest, particularly the whole of the Coast Range.

What had been a life-long struggle to coax a few miserable plants to grow in that hot, arid climate of the southwest turned out to be the opposite problem in the Pacific Northwest. Leave a bare patch of ground beyond two seasons and something will be growing on it voluntarily; more like expropriating the land, actually. Squatting, towards permanent occupancy. You have to beat back plant life, and continue to monitor captured territory, lest the natives, and in particular, the invasives, reoccupy the turf you'd only temporarily conquered. There are no permanent "victories" on the land, here, if by victories we mean something on the order of managing the land for human purpose, as distinct from maintenance of the natural order.

I'm guessing that's probably true everywhere given enough time (ok, not the Polar regions, not the Altacama Desert of Peru/Chile). It's conspicuously so here in the Northwest. The so-called natural order has got this drill down; been performing this Cycle of Life Show season by season, century by century, through millennia, at a geological pace. You wanna piece of the action, you better figure on defending what you think you can carve out, 'cause these locals aren't going anywhere, and they will be back to this little piss-ant patch you so audaciously claimed, just as soon as you turn your back on it for two consecutive seasons—unless you've poisoned it so thoroughly that nothing will grow.

As the days stretch out and the rain isn't so incessant, with warming sun breaks occurring between furious showers, the plants are a riot of competition against all the other plants in the vicinity for the available sun exposure, sufficient nutrient-adequate soil, and sufficient water access, especially in the dry months. Here, summer is extravagant when the woods are reborn, sprout, flourish and finally dry out from the seemingly endless drizzle and chill that confine us for too long. To People of the Desertlands, such vigorous, prolific, relentless vegetative growth came as more than a little intimidating.

Before emigrating from Arizona, I was inured to shades of earth tones without much leafy vegetation to contend with: Desert browns from light tan to a deep, wet clay that can be almost red. And the deep, cerulean skies. Browns and blues: I didn't think much about it. That's just how it was. But here, my God, the greens! I couldn't take my eyes off the layers of mottled, vertiginous growth. It was as if my eyes had been deprived of this array of hues, this portion of the spectrum. Even now, unwilled by my conscious mind, my vision seeks out the greens around me, feeds on them, drinks them in, the dappled layers of green beyond description, a balm for the retinae, a tonic for my withered, sun-baked and desiccated carcass.

A Yellow Submarine Précis

Were there to be guiding principles, an organizational vision to this social entity we'd just given a name to? Something to rally and motivate fellow communards in times of adversity? A mission statement, per chance? Ha! By all measures, the Sub crew were minimalist organizers and records keepers—to be euphemistic. Presumably, the general feeling was the less codification and paperwork, the better. Jes' go with the flow, bro. Stay loose; don't let yourself get pinned down. In terms of socio-economic theory, Yowie veered toward socialism when necessary, anarchy when possible. Still, he grappled with the ideas that might minimally bind them on behalf of the group.

One point was very important to him; he wanted the commune to commit to being inclusive, being at least in theory open to anyone who might want to join them, become a member, participate in their activities. Thoughts of exclusivity in one or another form were philosophically abhorrent to him. He couldn't abide being a part of yet another exclusive institution: Sorry, members only. No one presented any serious opposition, seeing no particular real-life application, one way or the other—to their eventual folly. Thus, the notion was adopted as their default social position. This suitably praiseworthy concept would come to haunt them in short order, whenever it came to defining/maintaining a group identity in the face of open-ended comings and goings.

At one point Yowie offered up for group review a brief statement trying to encapsulate a sense of responsibility toward each other. It went something like:

> *Rules are constructed and implemented*
> *only in the absence of people acting responsibly*
> *toward one another and the environment*

...and was received by widespread indifference.

He was trying to show that rules can be minimized, even theoretically abolished, to the extent the people in the community act in accordance with the interests of the whole over the individual and/or the few; thus, a heavy burden is incurred interpreting the word, responsibility. This vague concept (Act in accordance with the good of all) would work best—if it can work at all—in a small community where everyone knows and interacts with everyone else, like a commune.

Experiments like theirs were probably always special cases to the mainstream because beyond a certain population they would no longer be viable, and could not be used as a model to be projected onto the population as a whole, unless that society were willing to regroup into commune-like cells. The group that occupied the two houses, 25 people, at the high-water mark, was large and complicated enough that few resident-occupants would have wanted more people to live with, each with her/his unique personal needs and idiosyncrasies.

No Yellow Submarine Charter was ever written. That's too bad, actually. It would have been intriguing to examine/interpret the artifacts, to pour over the effects to help define them from the immediacy of the moment. Yowie's accounts, compiled in 1971 and '72 with Gina at Gull Haven, their coastal retreat, appear to be the nearest thing we have to documents from the period.

Finances

How would we make it; how were we going to pay the bills? Chanren came directly from a teaching job and put up first and last months' rent ($150/mo.). Among my worldly possessions in my backpack, I brought along $75 from a bad debt. Malcolm and Mudra had a $100/month stipend from the Resistance. Pollo was eking out on a school loan, and the rest came broke. One way our communal model worked was in the realm of household expenses.

In the pre-granola economy, costs could get negotiated but ultimately were divided by the number of Submariners per unit of time—at least monthly, to make rent and utility payments. Say, rent was $150, utilities together were $30, and incidental household expenses (soap, cooking oil, toilet paper, etc.) were $20. That's $200 divided by number of occupants; if we were 10 members, then each one's monthly nut would be $20. My $75 in mid-August lasted me until I got the cannery job in late-October. If you were willing to be careful, you could live on the cheap in Eugene, Oregon, in the fall of 1968. Needless to say, that was very different money from today's dollars. The minimum wage for Oregon in those days was $2/hour; virtually anyone could come up with $20 a month for living expenses.

I came across an interesting nugget while researching the minimum wage for the period. There was another graph superimposed on the same time line, demonstrating that the periodically adjusted "poverty level" came closest to intersecting the minimum wage of a 40-hour-per-week job in 1968/69. Needless to say, such a level of economic existence was nothing to aspire to, but aspirations aside, many of our fellow countrymen had no choice but to do the best they could eking out a "living" under such conditions. The point is, at no time before or since records were taken has the minimum wage approximated the amount of money required to maintain a poverty-level existence. At all the other recorded times a minimum-wage job was unable to provide, and fell short of a material existence at what the US Government defined as the poverty level.

What does this factoid tell us? Well, one possible interpretation permitted a relaxing of social constraints, some of which, in tougher economic times, would have been relegated to the Frivolous Fantasy Bin in deference to concerns about paying for food and rent, the necessities. It wasn't quite as difficult to get by, economically speaking, compared to times before and since. During this brief period, 1968 ~ '69, young adults had relatively more time/money/energy/freedom to flaunt political, esthetic and generational differences—to say nothing of increasing defiance of a mainstream undeclared war with a tiny country in southeast Asia, requiring an active conscription to feed that war machine.

When one is about to be thrust into a kill or be killed scenario in an unknown and heretofore unthreatening culture, one can be quite passionate, in league with others, in opposing the draft, the war, and the American government's commitment to pursuing the slaughter.

There's no direct causality tendered here, just an intriguing parallel between a laissez faire, general sense of prosperity (despite the War, early on anyway) in the one hand—as expressed by a minimum wage job permitting a poverty level existence. This corresponded to a social movement expressing a Do your own thing, let-it-all-hang-out unraveling of the social strictures, emboldened by the growing Resistance movement. The younger generation was often riotously participant in the public rejection/repudiation of the economic, political and especially military hegemony our kleptocracy seemed hell-bent on pursuing globally. The usual ruse of the war mongers was the imperative of America to act to prevent communist expansion (the latest iteration of "the domino effect," coined by Eisenhower's S of S, John Foster Dulles)—having the practical consequence of Southeast Asian mass murder on a huge scale—don't we call that genocide?

Meanwhile all around, happy-faced mainstream consumers wallowed in their newly empowered materialism here at home.

> *...Things fall apart; the centre cannot hold;*
> *Mere anarchy is loosed upon the world,*
> *The blood-dimmed tide is loosed, and everywhere*
> *The ceremony of innocence is drowned;*
> *The best lack all conviction, while the worst*
> *Are full of passionate intensity.*
>   from *The Second Coming*, W. B. Yeats

* * * * *

Another "event" taking place those years as a sub-rosa facilitator of more relaxed social norms across the board was the coming of age of the "baby boomers"—those born after World War II up to about 1964. The preponderance of this generation was Spock babies, and it troubles me to have to add this has nothing to do with Star Trek, or any such fantasy existence. Dr. Benjamin Spock, a pediatrician who'd studied psychoanalysis, revolutionized childcare with his best-seller, Baby and Child Care, published in 1946. In this book he persuasively argued for treating each baby/child as the unique human s/he is—to run the risk of over-simplifying. Yes, babies were trainable, and could be taught to eat and sleep on a schedule, for example. He was able to show, however, that babies raised more flexibly, case by individual case, in the long run became better-adjusted adults.

In short order the victors of WWII were persuaded to relax their Spartan/ Puritan/ Prussian values of Raise 'em to know hardship; a little deprivation/ denial is good for 'em; strengthens character!, to something a good deal more humane, if not indulgent. Leading, one supposes, in circuitous literary fashion, from Holden Caulfield of "Catcher in the Rye", to James Dean in "Rebel Without a Cause," and finally, Randle McMurphy, chief bull-goose loony of the "Cuckoo's Nest."

Dichotomies

Despite post-WWII prosperity and general well being America was, and still is, fractured into Apollonian and Dionysian camps, the Puritans vs. the Libertines. The Vietnam conflict only exacerbated the rift by emboldening the war resisters, young and disposed to self-indulgence, hedonists all, to get loose.

However, in order to better understand these sybaritic acolytes of Dionysus (God of wine, intoxicants, and the pursuit of Arts), it's only fair that we conduct a cursory examination of their counterpart, a view of the contrast, if you please. It is incumbent upon us to consider Apollo's archetypal representatives among us, here, in the land of the brave, home of the free, those often self-righteous proponents of "ol' time values" and "law'n'order" and "correct behavior," who crusade against sin and depravity—moral laxity—in all their nefarious forms. Who were those dudes?

Anthony Comstock fills the bill better than most. Ol' Tony, balding with some of the most luxuriant muttonchops going, was a Victorian prude who'd served as a young man in the Civil War without incident, except to take serious objection to the frequent use of profanity on the part of his fellow soldiers. If that were truly the case, he was doubtless invited to fuck himself, and anatomically challenging variations thereof proportional to his objections, without the slightest diminution of the offensive language. As a result, Comstock may very well have learned to bite his tongue, and pledge a private vow to take it out on the entire country at his earliest opportunity.

Lo and behold, by 1873, he succeeded in getting the Comstock Act legislated, which, among other things, forbade circulation of "obscene" literature (*guess who got to interpret that word?*) and articles for immoral use, including abortion devices, and contraception potions and literature: No reproductive choice for women on Comstock's watch! Wouldn't you know, his campaign had formidable church-based support—out of concern for the deterioration of public morals (*sound familiar?*). As a result of his 40-year reign of "holy" terror on personal freedoms as US Post Office Special Agent, he was said to have gloated over having sent thousands of people to prison—and driven no fewer than a baker's dozen to suicide. According to Eric Schlosser in *Reefer Madness*, Comstock was dismissive of his detractors: "No sect nor class has ever publicly sided with the smut dealer except the Infidels, the Liberals, and the Free-Lovers."

Toward the end of Comstock's rule, a young law student became his understudy, eager to learn Big Tony's organization, methods, range of targets, "artful" skirting of laws and the US Constitution, and other such useful skullduggery. That devious little shitweasel of a federal agent was none other than J. Edgar Hoover, soon-to-be Director-for-Life of the Federal Bureau of Investigation.

Another paragon of right-minded Apollonian "virtue" was Harry J. Anslinger, the Commissioner of the Federal Bureau of Narcotics from 1931 to 1962. Thanks to Du Pont Petrochemicals' urgings and William Randolph Hearst's rabid, yellow journalism, the Commish soon saw the light as to the growing menace of marijuana. This pathetic excuse for a public servant was willing to stoop to the most craven lies to dupe a naïve public, in order to protect us from ourselves. Try this whopper: "By the ton it is coming into this country—the deadly, dreadful poison that racks and tears not only the body but the very heart and soul of every human being who once becomes a slave to it... Marihuana (sic) is a shortcut to the insane asylum" (Wikipedia).

And in a highly propagandized article "Marijuana Assassin of Youth," he (sketchily) reports "A Chicago mother, watching her daughter die as an indirect result of marijuana addiction (vague enough for you?), told officers that at least fifty of the girl's young friends were slaves to the narcotic.

"No one can predict what may happen after the smoking of the weed... There must be constant enforcement and equally constant education against this enemy, which has a record of murder and terror running through the centuries" (*The American Magazine*, July 1937).

Thanks to that blind, authoritarian bigotry—once the menace was identified, and translated into policy and law by the ham-handed tactics of Anthony Comstock and Harry J. Anslinger under the guise of public defense and protection—tens of thousands of people's lives have been interrupted, damaged, and forever changed simply because they violated these medieval, arbitrary, and, in the case of marijuana, completely illogical strictures. Federal law continues to consider marijuana equivalent to methamphetamine and heroin—a "Schedule I controlled substance"—and many states continue to arrest, try, and incarcerate accordingly. As a result, the emergent Dionysian celebrants of the late-1960s had their own, ready-made institutional pariahs to mock and ridicule, to vilify and rail against. Thanks, Tony! Thanks, Harry! We couldn't have made up better foils. You virtually insured that legions of America's youth would become Lotus Eaters!

We were young, and the times provided a distinct choice. One end of the spectrum winked, beckoned, and did everything short of mooning us to coax us into choosing Be yourself, and Let it all hang out, and Turn on, tune in and drop out. The other side of the divide inveigled us to submit to the traditional, the safe, the tried and true. This side looked a lot like unquestioning Obedience to God and Country, and Guns and personal freedom uber alles. By the time I'd graduated from the U of A in late spring of '68—that's nine years for a BA Degree—I'd traveled to some 40 countries, including living in Greece over a year. For me the choice wasn't difficult at all.

It's just that a good deal of that Dionysian turf was a violation of the law of the land. It was definitely pushing the limits. There could be serious repercussions.

* * * * *

This book considers it relevant to explore Why as well as How this ambitious experiment took place, and not just detail its chronological events. I think everybody believes s/he lives for the most part consistently, that his/her life tracks some logic—of intent, if not entirely in fact. Science is said to order the observed data of experience, and to that extent, we are all "scientists." We rationalize (make sense of, ascribe meaning to) our own lives. This experience would be our attempt to construct a purposeful community specifically not based on social models we had grown up with and for the most part continue to surround us yet today.

With few exceptions, we were all from middle class, urban, WASP backgrounds: A yearning nation's blue-eyed pride. Our parents came out of that WWII-victor mindset. After having prevailed in that global abattoir, the world was their oyster. What could make us, independent of each other, be willing to give up the status, comfort, and security virtually handed us by our parents' generation, for an "alternative lifestyle" we knew nothing about and thus, were going to have to make up as we went along?

The merit-badge boy scout. The high school cheerleader. Surely the lure of unbridled promiscuity, of itself, was insufficient to induce all 30-or-so otherwise sane young adults over the course of two-plus years to forsake their homes, schools (*twenty years of schooling...*), jobs (*and they put you on the day shift*) to go off somewhere in the Oregon hills and live in sin and depravity in a hippie crash pad.

Not our Susie, with those dope fiends and sex maniacs, waiting to have their way with her, make her their sex slave, glands simply oozing in anticipation.

Not our Joanie—they smell bad, observe questionable standards of hygiene, won't shave, are disrespectful, won't work, and—they don't know their place.

Please, not Patty; she's only 17—all of them out of their minds on durugs, indiscriminately copulating like Bonobos, for crissakes.

The Honor Society student, well liked by his classmates. The university sorority girl, complete with make up and bleached hair, a veritable fashion queen destined for prestige and exalted social status, until... succumbing to... the diabolical lure... of... Freakdom!

By many measures, America had reached or was rapidly approaching its high water mark in economic, technological, and cultural influence on the world stage. Why, then, would we, the offspring of upwardly mobile parents in a still presumably upwardly mobile society, choose to forfeit all that "promise" and live at a lower socioeconomic level than we were presumably entitled to? For the record, I was able to account thirty adults over a two-year period from a detailed demographic tally. Sixteen of those adults twenty years old and older had at least BA Degrees, five of them reported having accomplished MA Degrees, and at least three had "postponed" pursuit of their PhDs. It's a safe bet this was a better academic ratio per adult population than the national average at the time.

> *Trade in your hours for a handful of dimes*
> *gonna make it, baby, in our prime*
> *get together one... more... time*
>
> *Five to One,* the Doors

At the time it might well have felt like we were renouncing that mindless, follow-the-leader lifestyle. At the time it felt like a permanent forfeiture. While much of what we championed got emasculated/commodified/co-opted/cheapened in the months and years that followed that "Counterculture Spring," a modicum of environmental sensitivity, and thereby conscience, did become part of the mainstream narrative. Recall, it was under Nixon's watch that Clean Air and Clean Water, as well as the EPA, got implemented. To your average "Free" Market resource plunderer in current times, that translates to "unwanted government regulations/restrictions." In those days clean air to breathe and water to drink still seemed worthy of safeguarding by governmental oversight.

The exploding counterculture movement could not have failed to empower a whole generation of healthy, curious young adults to experiment with different identities in unique contexts, for long enough and just so long. The fact that so few of our hard-fought campaigns of the day prevailed in the long run is perhaps a disappointment, from distant hindsight. Ah, but the consciousness raising—our own, as well as others—sure tasted sweet at the time.

from l. Chanren, Jeffrey, James, Pollo holding Gagutz, Yowie, May, Anita holding Karisma, Mudra, Malcolm, pregnant Doris, and Quarrel. Autumn '68. South presentation of the Sub.

On the floor, Jerry Ferrox playing w/ Gagutz, Marta reading *The Register-Guard* with Yowie, Chanren in the background, Nov. '68.

Mudra & Malcolm, foreground w/ Chanren background R. Autumn '68.

from l, Marta, Mudra, Tom blowing smoke rings, Gagutz in rapt amazement. Autumn '68.

The Digs

Our three-story, babyshit-ochre manse was located just below Florid Point, through Hendrix Park. We had five "private" rooms and two larger public rooms, in addition to a kitchen/dining combo. The up and downstairs "living" rooms were work and hangout areas in the daytime, especially on bitterly cold days with sheeting rain. Pollo had finagled an old wood-burning cook stove, which we set up in that living room and used regularly to help warm the room. We must've scrounged an overstuffed chair and somesort of garage sale misery sofa. Some of Pollo's fine arts grad-student sculpture added a little bohemian charm. Garage sale lighting and the de-rigueur sound system completed our parlor décor; ready to entertain polite guests, such as a clutch of Jehovah's Witless flies sensing a fetid den of heathens hungry for The Word.

Palms rubbed together, *Oh, do come in, won't you? We're so happy to meet you!*

From the front door entrance facing south into the house, one encountered the main living room with a private room off to the left (east), a room I occupied as soon as I arrived. There was a single mattress; I had a sleeping bag and a change of clothes. I was home free.

People more often than not hung out in the kitchen, the nexus of the house. Through a doorway beyond the living room lay the kitchen/dining area, taking up the width of the house. To the right (west) was the sink beneath a window overlooking a cement pad and outlying landscaping. Countertops and cupboards were arrayed on both sides of the sink, wrapping around to the stove on one side, the refrigerator the other.

The opposite end of the room had a window looking out the east side; left of that east view was the stairwell to the attic, an undivided space running the length of the house under the peaked roof. Next to the attic access was the door to the main-floor bathroom. The whole of the kitchen was clad in vertical knotty-pine siding. We quickly adorned the walls with posters of our icons: a young Janis in a saucy pose, a bottle of Southern Comfort on display, as I recall; the Stones with Brian Jones front and center, when they still cared enough to "dress up" for a photo shoot; Jimi, struttin' his stuff. Jim Morrison, I think. The Dead? Quicksilver? I can't recall who else completed our Pantheon, those select few who loomed over our deliberations.

The house came with a beat up, old picnic table complete with the attached benches, in lieu of a proper dining room set. Many an hour was passed seated at this wretched excuse for a table. It was a creaky, treacherous old pig. If one person, sitting opposite two or three others, decided to stand up suddenly, the whole shootin' match could flip ass over teacups, pandemonium ensuing. For the first year, it was here, at this miserable table, that we ate, smoked, argued everything from cosmology/theology to minutia, as in whose turn it was to muck out the bathroom (Care to guess which is the more important?), smoked some more, proposed plausible preponderances, badgered the cooks and other unwary passersby, and generally maintained the daily running narrative of the Sub—and in the meantime, inhaled a skosh more.

The third floor eventually became a dormitory with wall-to-wall mattresses, where sleep at night was emphasized, especially since there was no pretext of privacy. But in those first months it was Pollo's garret, the site where "le Picasso-esque artiste" conducted serial interviews for models; the very locus where initiation rites were performed on the college coeds. (One can only imagine the judicious application of his magic wand in such rites.) Gagutz, his five-year-old son, slept there also.

If it turned out that all the other "private rooms," all four of them, were occupied—for various consultations, laying-on-of-hands, Tantric/Priapic therapies, whatever it took—then one or the other living room would have do. If you could stay awake longer than the other late night revelers, then the room was "yours." It meant you often had to outlast Doctor John conjuring voodoo spirits into the wee hours: "Walk on gilly con-con, walk on gilded splinters…" wondering, What the shivering shits is that about? At the same time, Is it something I really want to know?

Nobody had morning shift, blue-collar working hours to keep, except for my brief cannery career. No reason not to stay up as long as the music's playing and someone can still roll joints; no reason not to sleep as late as you want. Except that Karisma, at 9~10 months, wasn't going to sleep late, no matter when you went to bed. Too soon, the music would resume mid-morning, and in any case, people were gonna be tramping around talking in normal voices, moving stuff, making noise. Might as well get up.

About 80 feet past the house on Florid Hill was a parking pad suitable for four or five vehicles. It soon became our parking lot of choice. Access from this parking site to the back door was via steps and a walkway that passed an 8' x 12' garden storage, or perhaps playhouse. It wasn't insulated but it was built to code with a big, south-facing window and a snug door. It didn't take long before Pollo had made it into a cozy little private quarters with an extension cord run from the back porch, and newspaper stapled between the joists/rafters for insulation.

The "barn" was an unfinished building 80 ft or so down the hill from the main house, on the 2-acre property. Prior to our renting the place the building had been used for storing hay for the neighborhood hobby horses and there was some left-over hay in the open "garage." This structure was part of our rented property. Intended as a separate apartment, it was in a state of construction limbo. It had been code-framed, roofed, and externally sheathed but unfinished internally, and was neither electrified nor plumbed. Perhaps most importantly, it had no doors or windows. That meant ambient temperature was the temperature "inside": quite cold in winter. But if your hormones made you intrepid enough and that's where a semi-private bed, at least covered from the elements, was available, that's where you hastened forthwith. Taking agonizing minutes of combined body heat to warm up the cocoon in the bed enough to take off clothes and get serious about some ol' give-and-take (or is it give-and-give?).

In the summertime, when people were on the move, and we had both more "members" as well as more "visitors," the barn became an auxiliary bedroom. By the second summer, we'd communized our neighbors, an all-American nuclear family: husband, wife, son, 9, and daughter, 10—and the population of the Yellow Submarine for a short time maxed at 25 "members," roughly translated by this time as resident and participant.

The problem was there was no central governing mechanism to decide stuff, like whether a freeloader should get the bum's rush. It was sort of Cooperate when possible, live and let live when not. Very anarchic. Except that one or more people with no place better to go, could, and did, worm their way into our good graces (the hallmark of a con artist?) and even after the shine wore thin, they remained fixtures because there was no authoritative body to adjudicate such issues.

In hindsight that lack of even a periodic administrative/governing body, presumably collectively empowered, along with our completely porous "skin" allowing virtually unrestricted comings and goings, were our urban commune's Achilles' heels. Both of them.

Food, and all that pertains

We employed essentially three strategies in order to provide for our sustenance. Primarily,
    1) we availed ourselves of USDA U-surplus Foods,
    2) we learned to be gleaners, in that first year anyway, and

3) we accepted the generous offering of purloined canned food ("sharing the profits") from our townie comrade, Tumor, who'd been for years bringing home as many as six cans a day, his bonus, in his lunch box from the local cannery, his seasonal place of employ. He had closets full of unlabeled cans of all sizes. Fortunately Tumor could read the code inscribed on the top; still, it wasn't uncommon to open what you thought would be peaches in a light syrup, salivary glands starting to sluice in delighted anticipation—to find pickled beets. Not entirely substitutable, for most purposes. His contribution to the Sub galley, strange as it may seem, ranked second only to Abandoned Foods in variety and volume.

In terms of gleaning, big machine harvesters leave a surprising amount of corn on the margins and here and there, knocked down but missed stalks with mature ears. The (only?) virtue of such machines is that they work very quickly; nobody ever accused them of being gentle or subtle. However, if the grower receives his quota from the harvest, why wouldn't he turn his fields over to gleaners of the community for the 2 or 3% missed by the Combine? We were among several people who collected gunnysacks full of ears of sweet corn. Besides eating fresh corn until we were sick of it, we shucked the ears, blanched, and quick-froze gallon freezer bags full in our rented walk-in freezer.

We also regularly picked fruit and nuts off the trees along the alleyways and streets of our well-born city, blackberries pretty much wherever they were allowed a foothold in late summer, which was everywhere—a roadside scrap of untended land, an "unimproved" lot, anyplace to send down roots. It looked like the Promised Land to my incredulous eyes; so much bounty for the picking! Gleaning food had simply never occurred to this Arizona ignoramus.

Usually, if you ask the owner, s/he will let you harvest what would fall on the ground and rot, anyway. The trick was finding the unwanted fruit just before peak-ripe when the fruit sugar attracts other "harvesters." Like yellow jackets, which tend to not take any shit off us big, klutzy, soft-skinned creatures, especially when they are feeding on juicy, ripe pears. We made plum, pear and apple sauce, pear and apple butter (spicier and cooked down more), and some jams, as well.

We made a big deal about our gleanings surely because there was a certain amount of shared, labor-intensive camaraderie that occurred, a bonding in collecting, cleaning and preserving the free harvest. But, with the exception of the one-time fresh corn harvest, most of what we put up, i.e., froze or canned, didn't stick around long, and never rose to the level of feeding the family more than a few odd meals. We came quickly to realize that a lot of time and energy goes into the final product of, say, a pint mason jar of plum sauce—to see it disappear in one pancake breakfast for a dozen hungry souls.

It was disillusioning, especially, when Freddy's, down the street, could set you up 24/7 with an unschooled-taste "equivalent" of sauce/jam/syrup—or virtually anything else—for cheap. The Combine could produce more of your food stock, cheaper and more "conveniently," than you and a whole team of devoted eager beavers could ever hope to produce. It's all very seductive. You'll never be able to compete with that conveniently located supermarket. Right up until the time when the semis stop backing up to the loading docks. But we don't want to dwell on that just now.

Early on, by October or November of '68, we qualified for Abundant Foods, a USDA administered distribution of surplus food stocks. The surfeit of subsidized mega-agricultural production, it was the backbone of the school lunch programs, as well as providing free, marginally nutritious food to many of the nation's poor. This Welfare program was a social service we could get into, and the amazing thing was we legitimately qualified. It instantly became our largest source of unprocessed food stocks. But, God, what a trip to have to wait in line for up to two hours surrounded by the truly needy. All those vacant eyes. That gaunt, lean and hungry look, and us, the "voluntarily unemployed."

To say nothing of maintaining an adversarial, oppositional stance toward the US government in most other instances.

The criterion for receiving this largess was having earned below a benchmark amount per number of household members. If you had 10 residents, you had to have collectively earned less than $458 per month, with $39 for each additional person allowable. Once you get into the ethos of accepting surplus food, denatured/devitalized though it might be, it was really a good deal. The normal attitude I encountered from officials dispensing the food was one of not questioning our right to collect it, as if by policy they encouraged recipients. There was a lot to shovel out the door.

By stark contrast, my mother never missed a chance to take me/us to task for accepting Welfare food. She thought it was demeaning, killed the incentive to earn it; that one should have to work to buy the food, or words to that effect. One conclusion from her thinking is if you were able to work but chose not to (and there weren't charitable, humanitarian, communitarian organizations around), you should starve. Screw the arts, I guess, which have a long history of failing to be self-sustaining, with very few exceptions. This from a woman who grew up in the Great Depression when there were no unemployment insurance, no federal guarantee on bank deposits, no welfare, no Aid to Dependent Children (until 1936). No social safety nets.

And then in WWII everybody experienced rationing of most essential goods. She frowned on handouts, period. Especially for the willfully unemployed. So, you ask, How came I to be her spawn? Except for the exigencies of paying the bills, I don't think I've ever felt a serious incentive to "earn a living." Sorry Mom! It certainly didn't hurt my pride to accept a legitimate share of America's agriculturally subsidized excess food stocks. Literally mountains of surplus grains, dairy products, eggs, and some meats, all production driven to the point of glut.

I recall a bountiful month perhaps the third or fourth time we came for our allotment. For 17 occupant/residents of the Sub that month, we wheeled away four or five shopping carts mounded with dried and canned food. Before we got the '46 International Harvester truck, we needed at least two vehicles, or more than one trip to haul all this food back to the Submarine larder.

It was mostly familiar fare—peanut butter in 5 lb cans, bleached-white flour/5 lb bags, rolled oats, cornmeal, rolled wheat, pinto/sometimes navy beans, rice, dried peas, raisins, butter, canned stewer hens, turkey, stringy beef (played-out milkers, doncha s'pose?), corn syrup, powdered eggs and powdered milk. Each person who qualified was entitled to one unit of these packaged goods. Was there once in a while honey? I think so, without any assurance. Then, there was the less familiar fare, at least in kitchens I was accustomed to and had heretofore eaten from: bulgur, lard, and 5-lb. blocks of "American Cheese."

What's "less familiar" about cheese? you're asking. *How bad could it be? More grisly than gorgonzola?* First of all we needed to establish if this material were animal, vegetable, or mineral, because frankly, it exhibited many of the characteristics of a petroleum product. A shiny, softer version of Bakelite in an ungodly orange. Does not seem to biodegrade. Insects know to stay the hell away. An engineered product not unlike Silly Putty that we seem more-or-less able to metabolize—if you are unfortunate enough to be so hungry.

But the real coup de grace of this largess from the American heartland was cans of glow-in-the-dark-pink mystery meat, less charitably referred to as garbage meat. The label proclaimed, if memory serves, among the litany of crypto-chemical alarms, in eye-strain print, contents of "beef and/or pork, and other assorted animal-origin floor sweepings, e.g., contributions from the Elks' semi-annual possum, coon and nutria hunts; poisoned sea gulls and pigeons from the municipal landfill; assorted discoveries of county roadside crews…"

Such an unearthly pink, it was practically iridescent. Believing, perhaps naively, it was somehow beneficial/nutritious, Nita developed inventive ways to prepare this pureed animal-protein bologna. Such as pan-fried one-inch cubes, added to a greased casserole of one of your standard starches: pasta, rice, or potatoes, in one permutation or another. Often with a lot of spices: black pepper, cayenne of some sort, and a presence from the rosemary, oregano, thyme family. And any other vegetables you could throw in; garlic and onions, if you please. (Really now, what entrée isn't enhanced by garlic and/or onions?) It was perhaps not a coincidence that about this time Peebo became a vegetarian; I'd like to think USDA mystery meat helped push him over the edge.

We've already established that "American Cheese" isn't really cheese; it follows that it doesn't really grate in a standard cheese grater, which instead gouges gummy blobs of the vaguely sticky gunk. With opaque premonitions, in hopes it adds something positive to the diet based on being fortified with eleven vitamins and minerals, you scrape off some of this gunk onto the top of your casserole before popping said unit into the oven. After baking that puppy for an hour at 375 degrees, a reasonably hungry group of folks can and did tuck it away. Especially if that was it as to the main course.

Ah, but what can you do with bulgur? It came in 5-lb bags, no recipes included. Once we realized it was a type of processed wheat to make it impervious (or unpalatable?) to vermin, we tried grinding it down to a coarse flour in our counter-mounted Corona hand-crank mill and adding it to normal wheat-flour recipes, or soaking it before cooking it like rice, simmering/ steaming it for a long time. A long time.

After much experimentation, we demonstrated we could cook it long enough/ soften it up enough to masticate it a little, and quickly swallow it, indicating a minimal edibility. Rendering it palatable, however, was another level of complication, one we essentially failed at, I'm sorry to say. You had to do something to this stuff; seriously dress it up in order to knock it down. Doubtless we were just not that hungry most of the time, and the usual condiments/sauces/spices were rarely sufficient. It wasn't foul tasting, mind you, just somehow a taste found wanting. No amount of lipstick and eau de cologne could make this pig more palatable. The dilemma haunts me to this day, Bulgur: Food for the truly desperate, kitty litter, or insulation?

* * * * *

Early on we were fairly successful at rotating chores among each resident, especially with cooking and kitchen clean up. With seven or more adults you could be cook or cook's helper one evening, and dish washer an additional night a week and eat with the service of a restaurant (with extremely limited fare) the other five nights per week. In principle, anyway. But, as we know through hard experience, some of us have a knack for carpentry, some for mechanicking. Some demonstrate a flair for the arts, some for cooking. To each of these and any other category you'd care to add (jaw jacking? logorrhea?), we need consider those humble souls who are lacking any apparent skill, and are often more of a detriment in the kitchen than if they didn't "help" at all. In a less benign age, such people would be taken for a nice long walk in the woods… Fortunately, Nita was very creative with our early food stores—her kitchen mantra was, When it comes to basic recipes there's a lotta leeway—and forgiving when it came to some of the males who were clueless in the culinary arts.

Anita's Tale:

Some things I recall from the Yellow Sub

One day, probably a week or two before Christmas, Cleda (a Springfield wife of an Albertson's butcher and mother of three children) came over to use our oven. Her oven was on the blink—or so she said. She had made 3-4 batches of cookie dough the night before. She came walking in, full of smiles, carrying the bowls of dough and proceeded to start her baking.

As I recall, it took several hours before the cookies were all finished. I'm sure they were well sampled by all the group. I'm not sure how many cookies she actually got to take home. It seemed like she enjoyed the life style, and probably would have loved the idea of moving in. However, as I recall, her husband wasn't so keen on our group.

One time we all decided to go to the coast for a psychological retreat of sorts. It was to be a 2-3 day trip. I was still nursing Karisma and foolishly decided it was okay to leave her with Cleda and family. Poor Cleda had to cope with a VERY unhappy baby trying to drink from a bottle and being unhappy about being away from her mom for the very first time ever.

I remember the look Karisma gave me when we went to pick her up after the retreat. She was probably 10 months old but the look she gave me could have killed!! It was a look that said, "Don't you ever do this to me again!!" I'm not sure what benefit everyone got out of the retreat, but I certainly learned a good lesson from Karisma!!

In January 1969 I remember going up to Seattle in the VW bus to visit Quarrel and Doris (maybe to see baby Luke). We got there fine, but some time later, learned that a big winter storm was moving into the whole northwest. We loaded up in the bus and started back to Eugene. The storm hit us part way home. It took us hours as we crawled along the freeway in ice and snow. We finally made it to Eugene late in the evening and got as far as the bottom of Hendrick's Park and could go no further. We parked the bus and everyone grabbed all our stuff and we walked in the dark up through the park and down the road to the Yellow Sub. I remember one of the guys carried baby Karisma through the snow.

It turned out to be a record-breaking snow storm. We were stranded in the house for several days. I remember some of the guys walking down into town after groceries and supplies until the roads were finally opened up again. It was our first winter in Oregon and we haven't seen one that bad since!!!

I remember getting eggs at a bargain price (maybe 10 cents a dozen) from an egg ranch. They were called "chex" because each egg had a slight crack in the shell, thereby making them unsuitable for retail sales. We would buy them by the box full—several dozen. One day Karisma was sitting in the sun room and she discovered the box of eggs. When we found her she was busy throwing the eggs one at a time and breaking them on the floor. Yikes!!

I remember we would take turns cooking the dinner meal. Wayne took his turn very seriously. He would get a cook book and read several recipes until he found one we actually had the ingredients called for. I was impressed with his turkey tetrazinni he whipped up. I'm sure he substituted the government canned chicken, but he made a big casserole that everyone ate and enjoyed!

One of the heart breaks for me was the endless stacks of dirty dishes. I would go to bed at night with the kitchen all clean, and then during the night someone would decide to cook or bake something. When I'd get up and go into the kitchen—there were more dirty dishes!! I'm sure several people were doing their fair share, but it never seemed like enough was getting done.

I remember Pollo trying to convince everyone to get on a macrobiotic diet. He would make big pots of brown rice and lots of vegetables. I'm sure it was healthy, but it just took some getting used to.

I remember out bedroom was a tiny room down on the bottom floor. It had no door, just a curtain hung for some privacy. At times there might be 4-5 people sleeping in the next room when I'd get up in the morning. This was a VERY small room with just enough room for our mattress and the baby crib. There was a ceiling to floor window in the room that looked over the garden and down the hill.

One of the things I struggled with was the constant fear of being busted. If we were all busted I being a mother was putting Karisma in real jeopardy. I feared she could be taken away from us. I had heard that the cops would do raids early in the morning. I would wake up and if it was a tiny bit daylight I would look out that big window and check to see if I might see cops ready to bust the commune. I was going to be the early warning system! Thankfully it never happened!

(Yowie resumes) The galley cooks often made bread, to varying degrees of success. It was a good way to use up the denatured white flour, and other Abundant Foods grains, once ground in our handy countertop-mounted, hand-crank Corona grain mill. If you observe some basic notions about yeast, water, flour, kneading, and temperature, it's hard to screw up edible fresh-baked bread. Yowie learned a basic bread recipe from Pollo in those early days, and continues to use a variant to this day.

Through their early baking prowess, on one conspicuous occasion, inadvertently, they were able to create some kitchen "art." Someone—the perpetrator is lost to history, Yowie would cop to it if he were the agent—had some loaves that were taking their sweet time rising. Or this person was in a hurry and thought they had risen enough. Or had forgotten any yeast at all. Anyway, said loaf (only one survived) had been abandoned in the oven in at least 300 degrees for many hours, baked very much in the manner of a brick.

Once discovered and cooled down, they faced the conundrum of what to do with it. Using conventional cutlery was ill-advised; they could've cut it on a table saw, but to what end? Nobody was willing to break teeth to eat it. Even if we'd reground it and sprinkled it over our granola, there were no longer any nutrients extant. By the fourth or fifth hour of carbonization, such components of nutrition had passed up the flume. Gone. A door stop? Perhaps, but towards its highest and best use, one enterprising culprit/ phantom artist (Who knows? Perhaps it was the baker! With the hammer!) drove a 6" spike through the "loaf" and into a chunk of 2x6, sawed off about a foot long, and mounted it on the wall, where it remained for quite a while. The whole works probably should have gotten a coat of clear varnish, but it seemed impervious to mold without it. It remained a wall decoration, right up there with our pantheon of rock icons, for something like a year.

* * * * *

In addition to the sustenance that keeps life and limb together, is the food for the mind. The winter of '69/'70 was an intermittent social trauma with volatile egos bouncing off the communal walls, angry words behind closed doors. To be sure, reefer is a great elixir here, a moderator, especially in winter. Prevalent and fairly cheap in that buzz-for-buck ratio, our Patrona, Lady Maria Juana was a frequent, if not constant, companion. She's something of a euphoric, heightening sensory experiences of all stripe. LSD makes the sense of confinement/separateness go away—along with the rest of your personal identity—but more about the noble acid later. Cheap booze sometimes "helps," though more often than not, with more dire consequences. We were lucky to not have any resident hard-core juicers.

* * * * *

Tumor taught Yowie a quick and simple homebrew recipe he'd used for years, and they quickly got into a routine of cranking out five-gallon lots of cheap "house beer." They needed equipment; Tumes had stashed a bunch of quart beer bottles (in the days before twist offs), a bottle capping press, a gross of bottle caps, and a hydrometer, to measure the amount of sugar (in solution, hence denser than plain H2O) that gets converted to alcohol and CO2 by the yeast. He still had an ax handle with the shellac dissolved from the business end, from years of stirring the wort. Beer yeast was basically a one-time cost, since after bottling the first batch, we'd collect some of the yeast dregs from the bottom of the plastic garbage tub to tuck in the back of the frig as a starter for the next batch. Other one-time expenses: about 7 ft of 3/8" thin, clear-plastic tubing for siphoning the finished aerobic fermentation into the bottles. And a cheap plastic 8~10 gallon waste bucket—what could go wrong with plastic? Silent Spring had not yet penetrated the consciousness of the Yow-meister, who'd never heard of toxic bis-phenols, phthalates, and other exotic petroleum byproducts found throughout the food chain. What, me worry?

They had to pay real $ for malt syrup and sugar, both cheap, from the supermarket until Food Stamps took the place of Abundant Foods. When Food Stamps was implemented a year or so later, the Sub brewers were finally able to "buy" all the ingredients for a finished homebrew with Gummint scrip, a milestone they were proud of. Food Stamp money would not permit the outright purchase of alcohol, but would provide for ongoing expenses in the manufacture of some damn fine grog, by wide acclaim. It was slick; for a while there, they'd make a new five-gallon batch every two weeks. One week to ferment it and an antsy week to "age" it (let the yeast mostly settle out) before drinking it. If they had their ducks lined up, by the time they'd finish one batch, another would be aged to perfection, scratch that, drinkability, and one about ready to be bottled. Masters of zymurgy they were not. Still, life was good!

Having simple beer fermentation down emboldened them to try some fruit wines; why not? Like beer, it's a variation of yeast, water, sugar, and the source of the flavor: berries, fruits of any imagined type, and, yes, even flowers. Dandelion wine was the Sub's biggest fermentation heartbreak. The inspiration came from a growing concern for the pantry space devoted to

USDA corn syrup, coupled with a recognition of the adjacent unmowed field as a sea of golden Dandelion heads rippling in the breeze. Their simple recipe required quite a lot of blossoms for a five-gallon batch, so it was necessary to muster the usual layabouts to the task.

Six or so people to share a project with can sustain one's interest for some time, even though the task is menial/repetitive. During all of fifteen minutes the novelty of the experience, and the others' impressions of the experience, was thoroughly engaging. Eventually, though, as the pillowcase begins to show some heft, the perceptions shift rather quickly to the event as no fun at all, entirely too field hand menial, even burdensome. You begin to question yourself if this labor is going to be worth it. For the next twenty minutes it's a full-on duel between the opposing sides, each able to score points but neither able to win the argument. In such a trajectory it's easy to see how some among the core flower pickers might be little more than going through the motions by the end of that first hour of Dandelion harvesting.

After what seemed like a long time (for the chronically indolent), the reapers returned with the bounty: two more-or-less full pillowcases. But then came the time for the real labor: the golden flowers had to be separated from the green stalk and backing, Ugh! This chlorophyll matter easily made up ¾ of bulk of the flowers. Plus, it was practically impossible to remove all the material… Painful hours later the team, muttering dark epithets under their breath, completed separating most of the flowers, which were then steeped into a giant tea with boiling water, to which we added a great deal of the corn syrup, and stirred it until dissolved in solution. By the time it has cooled to 70~75 degrees, it was time to add the yeast.

Two days later it was pretty clear something was wrong. We'd done everything according to instructions, being genuinely motivated to have this work. The yeast simply hadn't taken off; there were no little bubbles—let alone a thick foamy head—to signal yeast microorganisms beginning to consume the sugar in solution and excrete alcohol and CO2. (*Isn't it wondrous how one creature's poop is another's elixer?*) The temperature was within normal range. The assembled vintners uttered prayers—or were they imprecations?—to Dionysus, gave the wort a vigorous stir, and covered the crock for another few days. Had we allowed too much green material to taint the batch? Perhaps, but all agreed this outcome should not have stuck the fermentation; if anything, the minute amounts of stalk and green flower backing could have imparted some bitterness to the final taste, but not interrupted the process altogether.

No, indications were beginning to point to our choice of sweetener. So, what the hell is corn syrup, anyway? A basic ingredient in pecan pie and many recipes of candy, it certainly is sweet enough. There must be seven or eight molecular variations of "sugar." Hoorah for maltose, the sugar from malted/caramelized, sprouted barley (not particularly sweet to my taste); the toasted ingredients of your favorite tall, cool, frothy beverage, and choice of connoisseurs since Pharonic times. Fructose is the sugar from ripe fruit—and vegetables, like beets—the raw ingredients of virtually all wines. Through heavy processing/refining of natural sources we obtain sucrose. Also: Dextrose, lactose, and glucose, and perhaps others.

No doubt, there are yeasts that will, if given the chance, delight in gorging on the natural sugars they have adapted to, but might not like/know what to do with other configurations of sugar. Be it known, whatever fiendish brand of "sugar" corn syrup exemplifies (a corn-and-petroleum distillate?), the humble, all-purpose wine yeast they used was not having it, made the tragic decision to commit seppuku en masse, instead. Two weeks later, with nothing growing despite our futile efforts, we flushed the inert lot down the toilet. The Yellow Sub vintners—Tumor, Yowie, Carissima, et al.—were humbled by this abject failure to make Dandelion wine, and presumably know to never try that again. They did, however, go on to make some passable blackberry, and apple wines with good ol' cane sugar.

Hendrix Park

From the Sub to the Main Gate of the U of O—the other side of campus from us—was a good mile, maybe a little more; many of us regularly walked to town since our few vehicles were often employed in tasks to facilitate their owners. Until the Mamarone, we didn't really have a communal vehicle. Between our "anchorage" (to begin perhaps to abuse the sea-faring metaphors) and town was Hendrix Park, about a quarter mile from our front door.

Our local city park, from the perspective of this Arizona rube, was an amazing mix of a manicured Rhododendron and Azelea gardens in a White Oak grove, mature Doug Fir here and there, quite a prominent rose garden, picnic pavilion, kids' playground, a labyrinth of trails, and some Frisbee/play areas. During phases of the spring/summer, roses would be in bloom, along with the Rhodies, Azaleas, all a riot of colors. Dazzling pinks, reds, yellows, all the way to some ostentatious purple Rhodies I thought of as the painted ladies of the botanical realm, a trifle too garish to be natural. All of which stood before a background of a lush profusion of greenery.

There must be bunches of near-town hilltop "parks" in Arizona, but nothing like our neighborhood Hendrix Park commons. I was starting to come to terms with how profoundly different the climate—the amount of rainfall—was from anything I'd ever experienced, other than in travels. Just plain ol' H2O as the single most important variable. In a southern Arizona desert you might find five or six different native plant species on an acre of land. In western Oregon it wouldn't be too surprising to find five or six distinct botanicals per square-fornicating-meter!

On decent days the park would be the first choice for a walk. As we got familiar with the park boundaries and undeveloped private properties, we could follow semi-established trails south out of the manicured area and into pretty undomesticated land. Private homes hugged Florid Hill Dr., above as well as below the road, but started to thin out by our domicile. If memory serves, we could cross the street from our house, skirt a property, then immediately we'd be in brushy sloping hillside land not maintained. On dry days we could get to the park without having to take the road in front of our digs. That dense woody area was also occasionally useful when pressing assignations were in the offing and no private space available.

Our neighborhood park was simply a well kept/cared for city park in an urban center in Oregon; it had its own unique layout but was otherwise essentially duplicated in other Oregon cities. Its most distinguishing feature was not the flower gardens, or the mature stand of Doug Fir and Oak, or the fact that it lay along a ridge of a set of hills, or even the public facilities. For the first several months of the Yellow Submarine's existence Hendrix Park was home to a full-grown Roosevelt Elk, a five pointer, if memory serves.

I can't recall the dimensions of his confinement but they can't have been big, perhaps 25 x 40 feet. We'd go to pay our respects now and then to this magnificent creature. I don't think human visitors fazed him one way or the other anymore; he was inured to us, generally lethargic and disgruntled, as I suppose any sane beast would be in his predicament. Except for rutting season—late-September to early-November. Anyway, that was Bully's schedule. He could make the most mournful bugle calls late at night when all the city noises have quieted down. At such an occasion, you could suspend belief of where you were, and when, and almost imagine you were in some western Oregon forest a century before, with a randy bull elk a few hundred yards away, trying to whistle up a little romance:

Yo, some of you bad girls out there! I know you are there, because you are smelling soo-o goo-od! Don't you be coy, now. This ain't no time to be shy. Jes, bring it on home to Poppa...

You know, there probably were some elk cows occasionally within hearing range. It would have meant a mile or more of uninterrupted exposure and vulnerability to get to him, even at night. Open streets and fences. Cars and dogs, to say nothing of his enclosure. Invariably those cows got lured into harems in wilder, safer areas. Poor ol' Bully.

And then he got shot! I was incredulous. I could not understand how someone could get drunk or otherwise intoxicated enough to think s/he was killing this game animal in the wild, i.e., actually hunting. What satisfaction could the "hunter" take away from the experience? Except for climbing over a rather high cyclone fence—which he did not do—he wasn't going to bring home any of the meat, or the trophy head. The act was a complete waste. For years that deed ranked fairly high on my list of most senseless, idiotic acts of destruction. But a strange thing has happened: Without really being conscious of it, I've come to have some sympathy for Bully's killer.

It's not too much of a stretch to see Bully's life as unrelenting solitary confinement with hardly enough space to walk, impossible to run, sometimes the butt of taunts, pelted by rocks—tortured by sensory deprivation, a stultifying existence. He was able to detect different smells on the breeze, but most of them were effluents of petroleum combustion. Every other sensory input was blandly routine, even the food. Would Bully have offed himself, with a little more self-awareness (say, that of your average 7th grader), and access to a 9 mm handgun? Oh yeah, and an opposable thumb and some fingers?

Maybe Bully's capacity for boring caged life was greater than we humans can imagine—as opposed to execution, I mean. All of which presumes human sensitivities/awareness in the brain of this wild forest ungulate. Anyway, somebody may well have played Chief Broom to the lobotomized Randle McMurphy in Kesey's Cuckoo's Nest, and put Bully "out of his misery." The deed was done; I never heard whether the culprit was found. No more eerie, forlorn bugling in the night, and the neighborhood took another step towards civilized mediocrity.

Except for us, of course.

Clash of the Suitors

Pollo and Jerry Ferrox were each vying for the fair Sadie's carnal attentions. Jerry, a friend from town, "happened" to pop by for a neighborly smoke and some conviviality on the precise occasion Pollo was hosting the comely lass in question in his boudoir, upstairs. But even a floor away, Jerry's presence was providing too much of a distraction for Pollo to "complete the interview," so to speak. So he stomped downstairs presuming to evict Jerry from the premises. The man had been a well-behaved guest and nobody else there in the living room thought he should go. No matter, Pollo, shy a good foot of Jerry's height and maybe 2/3 his weight, set about trying to brow-beat/cajole him into leaving. Nobody would say that the riled Pollo wasn't feisty.

Truth to tell, the young lady was probably dismayed at having to choose between them, and had been doing quite well up to that point alternating between them, doubtless seeing other young bucks on the side. Yowie was around a little while Pollo was initiating the dance with her. She was so-o ripe that she exuded a Renoir, or Reubens-esque archetype of voluptuousness. To be sure, the bedroom eyes helped. If Yowz had sensed a shot at her, any pheromones directed his way, he would have been all over it; she could give your libido a run for it. But hard-fought battles of exclusivity almost never came to a good end. Surely not in those days. Too much hormonally driven manly pride on the line…

Well, the great battle, with much bluster and show, took place in the Sub living room, two snorting and bellowing bulls charging each other, two gladiators battling for the right to continue to slip between those creamy thighs. It was over quickly, resulting in some damaged furniture, and minor wear and tear on the combatants. Fortunately, no weapons were involved; it was mostly wrestling maneuvers with a punch thrown here or there. Having it transpire in front/all around you, while not at all knowing how far this would go was quite exhilarating, in not such a good way. Were they going to seriously hurt one another? Or more to the point, were they apt to injure a bystander? Yowie really didn't want to intervene.

Sometime afterwards, it is believed the combatants made up, but it's worth noting that Jerry got the goil. By and by she became Sadie Ferrox.

The Yellow Sub Cottage Industry

It was probably in anticipation of that first Renaissance Faire, the realization that we could have a booth, just by being us!—if we had something to present to the public for sale, anything (licit) at all. That last little part was indeed problematic, however, since we were your average feckless, indolent, slovenly, desultory, shiftless, layabout hippies, malingerers to a person, with no apparent skills anyone was willing to admit to. But Anita, bless her heart, must have seen a glimmer of promise, a potential for productivity that the rest of us, ourselves, were oblivious to—just the act of writing the word, productivity, gives me an involuntary shudder.

With the event scheduled less than a month away, there was no time to lose. Pollo volunteered to make a huge vat of hearty soup, to serve at the event with a chunk of decent bread, thereby cleverly sidestepping Anita's plans for the rest of us lumpen folk, for whom evidence of an artistic tendency was yet dormant, gestating, or DOA.

In short order she had us making patterns for neckties, vests, handbags out of newspaper. Then she'd enlist a cadre to raid the various clothing/material outlets for remnants of the gaudier stuff. Let's face it, sometimes the conventional standards of fashion no longer applied. Or maybe just got radically reinterpreted. And wouldn't you know it, this was just such an occasion. The rule this fashion cycle was there was no such thing as too tacky, or too tasteless. Material and color clashes that threaten ocular damage? The more flagrantly bizarre, the better! Once the material was accumulated and sorted for maximum retinal abuse, we would cut the remnants according to the desired pattern and sew it up.

It was like a real-life sweatshop except I think we only had one sewing machine. Everybody took a turn; I cranked out five or six passable ties towards the greater accumulation to offer to our astonished customers. We also produced some "colorful" vests and belts for the fashion-deranged guys and gals, and I think, handbags. Not a big fan of petroleum fibers: rayon, nylon, acrylic, or your five-pound-test fishing line? Precisely the blend for a natty sash! Or a chapeau that commands attention.

All goods hand made by living denizens of a hippie commune
was the implied sign at the sales counter. You know, support your local freaks/handicapped.

I remember harvesting black walnuts, drying them, and then sawing them very carefully with a coping saw into button segments, and yes, I still have all five digits on both my hands, thank you. I could get four big buttons and two little end pieces out of one nut. Once I'd cleaned, sanded, and oiled them—at least an hour per set—they made fine, decorative buttons.

Hand made! For you! Special price! $1 the set! You espeek Engleese? Crafted in our own little maquiladora, there on the other side of Hendrix Park.

Another craft we played around with was macramé. You start with three miles of fairly stout string (the stouter the cord the fewer the knots per square anything, an operating principle you grasp surprisingly quickly), and find something rigid—a gnarled tree branch, a quaint lampshade, anything to tie from. Then, with the patience, over-taxed eyesight and dexterity of a fine watchmaker, and the knowledge of knots of an old-school sailing salt, you make patterns in the string according to the placement and choice of decorative knots.

Nothing to it! Let your imagination run rampant! Except it took an incredibly long time to complete a single macramé project: days for something simple, weeks for an elaborate work. And they didn't sell well. More accurately stated, they didn't sell.

As near as I can tell from the benefit of considerable hindsight, the principle purpose to pursue macramé is not profit, but a kind of trance-like Zen meditational mind-out-of-body experience that can happen while your hands perform anything routine for any length of time, certainly repetitive knot-tying. Otherwise, outright begging would clearly have yielded a better nickels-per-hour ratio than sales of our one-of-a-kind, fine macramé objets d' art.

Since we didn't have a retail outlet for our wares we were beholden to the likes of Be-ins and Fairs like this one. I seriously doubt if we ever made any money from these labors, beyond paying for the staging of the event. Because of this pretext, however, we had a great time at Eugene's first couple of proto-Country Fairs. And developing some skill at one or more of those crafts didn't hurt anything, either. All of which boosts the importance of the granola economy to the Yellow Sub, when we finally put that together. Though no one would have admitted it at the time, we were very lucky Gina and Carissima recognized the opportunity and got us going on it.

The Pull to Pair

Marta and I became a couple when she moved in mid-November. She had an easy-going disposition, on top of being exotic-gorgeous, with cascades of bright-red hair and skin the color of whipped cream. We met at one or another of the Eugene Resistance events. Marta had an interesting sense of patriotism. She was disposed to appreciate the anti-warrior, over the traditional "war hero." It was an expression of her patriotic duty to think kindly of deserving young men who courageously stood up to the war machine. I was principled and articulate enough, and could demonstrate some bona fides in the struggle to end the Vietnam War—and more to the point, I could see a glad eye when she shot me one. It was not the first time that'd happened to me, but it was quite a pleasant discovery. Not that she wasn't quick to discern my sterling qualities…

There was a ferocious mutual attraction but, alas, it was not exclusive on my part. She ultimately wanted a monogamous relationship, and I'd just come out of a "failed marriage" in Tucson. It was the wrong time and definitely the wrong place for me to be serious about another mate relationship for long. Perhaps I gave her the wrong impression—said things she wanted to hear—because I really did enjoy being with her. Mea culpa.

So here's a little kick-in-the-crotch, self-induced retribution for you: When Marta had had enough, she found a small apartment in town and moved out, must have been summer of '69. I was stunned that she would leave this no-good, philandering snake and head out on her own. Talk about timing, ol' Tom Cherrytree, housemate of Quarrel and Doris in Seattle and recent arrival, was on hand to help her move out of the Sub and offer consolation her, as it were.

Abandoned, distraught, I wound up camping on the back porch of her new rental down toward campus in hopes that she'd take me back. I must've stayed parked on her back deck 40 hours leaving only to use the john at the service station at the corner. Needless to say, Marta wasn't having any of it, but she didn't call the cops on me; I'll say that much for her. In retrospect it all seems a little creepy, but at the time it took me most of two days to accept that she'd moved on. And while I surely deserved to be dumped, it smarted just the same.

This experience was a chance to see the dichotomous, perhaps hypocritical nature of my desires. Through the one hand, I professed interest in polyamorous relationships in a loving, caring environment. I pursued communal life more or less in this domain until I painfully discovered my own possessive/exclusive one-sidedness. This woman I was romantically attached to—just not exclusively—gave up on me entirely, and danced off to someone else's passion. Were my indefensible expectations flying in the face of many generations' worth of programming, to the effect that stable/good societies are composed of nuclear/extended families? Or simply the result of my own narcissistic desires? Male-Chauvinist Pig, c'est moi? I wanted a harem and nobody was cooperating!

* * * * *

From Marta's arrival the Sub saw no more additions until mid-March 1969. Winter attrition accounted for the departure of the Livingston nuclear family by the end of December. After a lifetime of sunny winters in central Arizona, the seemingly unrelieved dreary days in these environs can weigh on one. Anita and Karisma left at the end of March, but only to move a mile or so away. From that point until mid-June we took on five new members: Rick Porter, for six weeks; Lindy Button, ringleader of four other siblings who came to live with us, one year seven months; Gale, nine and ½ months; Terra, who left the Sub with Chanren, six months; and Geary Button, Lindy's older brother ex-military, leaving with Gale after seven months. Though most of these folks were fairly short term, they fattened up the ranks considerably, enriching the lives of the others, if making life more complicated at the same time.

> *Love is but the song we sing and fear's the way we die*
> *You can make the mountains ring or make the angels cry*
> *Know the dove is on the wing and you need not know why*
> *C'mon people now, smile on your brother*
> *Everybody get together, try to love one another right now...*
>
> *If you hear this song I sing, you must understand*
> *You hold the key to love and fear all in your trembling hand*
> *Just one key unlocks them both, it's there at your command*
> *C'mon people, smile on your brother*
> *Everybody get together, try to love one another right now.*
>
> *Get together,* The Youngbloods

From l. Tom, Chanren and Yowie on the trip to the Southwest.

The Reconnaissance/Recruitment Trip

After the Holidays, and in the doldrums of late winter in the early part of 1969, Tom, Chanren and I decided to embark on a road trip back to visit old friends, and dry out a little. Let's face it, if there is a time when warm and sunny Arizona actually attracts, at the same time cold-clammy, moldy-wet Willamette Valley blows, that period would likely be in the February-through-April range. Tumor and I must have been recently laid off from the cannery and flush with cash, and while I didn't think about it at the time, Chanren must have been in the early stages of disengaging from Anita. We just slung sleeping bags and a change of clothes in the back of Tom's VW Hatchback and headed south.

We must have been gone several weeks but I can't remember money ever being an issue. I don't think we ever stayed at a mo/hotel; we drove until we hit a city where we could connect with a friend or locate the local Resistance House—always good for a referral to a sofa and/or a floor to crash on. It was this subculture network. We were verifiable personages from the Eugene Resistance, and hospitality was extended/ reciprocated to fellow travelers.

San Francisco had moved on from the Summer of Love—which was no doubt a blessing. Notoriety, and the freeloader/scammer parasites had trashed every last inclination towards Fraternite, Egalite, and a community of sharing, while pursuing Liberte to its logical conclusion. Except for those cast-in-ferroconcrete institutions in existence since long before that Summer of Love, the Haight had been gutted. Those who had participated in/benefited from the '66~'67 phenomenon and still had hope, imagination and a social conscience had fled—to Marin County and points beyond—leaving the place to the zombies. It had been almost two years and the change was disturbing, shocking.

That first night I think we crashed at the Palo Alto Resistance Center, narrowly missing David Harris, an early inspiration to me when he came to the U of A to raise consciousness about the war—while acting student body president of Stanford. He must have caught me at the right time, because his simple, direct, eloquent message, that spring 1967 day, of taking responsibility for the war turned my head from mildly concerned/ functionally apathetic to fully engaged and committed to the Resistance. I'll bet David Harris helped radicalize a lot of people that spring.

Everyone chipped in for groceries, beer, and wine. Everyone shared what they had. There was an immense amount of camaraderie helping each other, in contrast to the dog-eat-dog out there—a real dichotomy of insider/ outsider, us vs. them. It was the solidarity of opposition to the Vietnam War, conscription/Selective Service, war profiteering, Merkan Imperialism—you get the idea.

We drove straight through from Pale High to Pheenicks stopping for piss breaks, coffee and cheap grub, in short, refueling us and the machine. Chanren and I both had valid driver's licenses and were prepared to relieve our intrepid chauffeur for an hour or two of shuteye. Tom, however, must have been channeling Neal Cassidy, driving essentially the entire distance, there and back. Cassidy, of course, was Kerouac's madcap partner and inspiration in On the Road, as well as Kesey's driver of Further on the cross-country bus trip that Kesey and the Pranksters made from the Left Coast to NYC in 1964. Ol' Neal was the most prominent and celebrated character to make the transition from the Beats of the 1950s to the Hippie counterculture of the mid/late-'60s, until his death in 1968.

I don't recall the sequence of friends we stayed with: the Tracers in Tempe/Phinx, Jose and Augusta, Double T and Gina in Tucson, Tumor's sister and her husband in L.A. on the way back, and probably others. It was hang out with each set of friends a few daze, occupy ourselves while these people attended to their scheduled obligations, and pursued more serious dissolution on evenings and weekends. Ned and Dana were welcome participants. And Bradley Littlefield, fearless, brilliant, laser-like mind, a gentle and kind soul, and the heart of the Tucson Resistance, was a fellow reveler.

I have a letter from Brad, postmarked Tucson, AZ, March 28, 1969—a month or so following our trip to the Southwest. As a further glimpse of the lives and times, I include it in full, starting with the envelope, a six-cent stamp affixed. In the upper left corner, from: The Crimson Crusader (see the back), 623 E. Helen St., Tucson, Az. In the center of the envelope, To: Yowell Mebsanuri (chief protector of the sacred fire), Yellow Submarine (most deadly, awesome, fear-inspiring, death-dealing instrument of war know to man), 2449 Floral Hill Dr., Eugene, Oregon. Left of the address with a dotted arrow leading to Yellow Submarine is a picture of a flower, S-attached to indicate plural, presumably, the peace sign, Love, & all the other good things to the righteous sailors of the intrepid…arrow.

On the back of the envelope: Deep in the bowels of Tucson, fabled city of gold lost in the past of archeological times, dwells the foe of all Bourgeois Evil, tireless fighter for socialist good, that mighty superhero who strikes fear into the hearts of capitalist, imperialist, aggressor pigs and their running dog lackeys everywhere, <u>The Crimson Crusader</u>. This, then, is a message from him. "Revolution is the best education for honorable men," Che. "Learn by doing," Amos Throop, founder of Cal Tech.

The letter itself reads:
Dear Yowie,
Glad you were able to put the kazoo to good use. May its sacred, supernal vibration resonate through the cosmos,

dissolving the unity of good & evil, to bring you the sublime benefits accruing to one who possesses so puissant an artifact. Right?

Still waiting to go to jail (any day now, any day now), as always. Trying to think what the hell I'm going to do after I get out. I just went through another identity, i.e., anthropologist. So far I've exhausted physics, biology, chemistry, math, the revolution, religion, anthropology, and being a bum. I'm reading Erickson's book, <u>Identity: Youth & Crisis</u>, and he talks about these pre-psychotic dudes who, during a period of crisis, spend all their time reading. Not too encouraging. One of the worst things about jail, I'm afraid, is that it will postpone for years my actually <u>doing</u> something. Such an idiotic, infantile obsession, this need to perform, but it is one common to the species, I'm informed by Erickson and Fromm. So, having been sanctioned by Authority, I shall continue my search for an occupational role. Lemme see, there's engineering, sales, economics, philosophy, agriculture…

Same scene around here. Jose still swearing he's going to drop out, Augusta still working, shuffling and shucking, Double T still studying for his comps, Gina's lugging books for the kids, Drew's looking for the Revolution, I'm on the pavement thinking 'bout the government, and throughout all of Maggie's Farm, the merciful arms of Big Mama Grass embrace us to her big Nirvanic breasts.

Would like to write something life-affirming, but seem to be trapped in the mood of the previous sections. Babies popping out here like corks in a champagne factory during an earthquake. Nextdoor neighbors had a kid. Helen Herschel is pregnant, Roxanne, Drew's old girlfriend is pregnant. Donna Branch just had another kid, and so on.

Well, time to consume another book. Keep on trucking.

Love,

Brad

The jail he blithely refers to is his looming stint in a federal pen, punishment for refusing induction--and wearing a second-hand store Army coat with a sergeant's insignias still attached, of all things. In the letter, he is in "jail" before he even starts his formal jail time. I don't think there is much of a correlation between reading and psychosis, but some fourteen years later the insatiably curious, peripatetic mind of Bradley Littlefield had seen enough.

He hanged himself from his bedroom door. I'm told, coats are hung, people hanged.

* * * * *

With the exception of Tom's sis and her straight hubby in The Angels, everybody had a stash of reefer, if not some 'shrooms or other psychedelics, and were only too happy to share. Peyote wasn't illegal yet, but ingesting it, eg., getting it past the ol' taste buds, especially fresh, was a really punishing way to access the mescaline. Our Too-sun and Pheenucks hosts had Mexican grass, fairly crude and seedy but cheap at $12 to $15 a lid (-/+ an ounce, often as not stuffed in a Prince Albert tobacco can). For Chanren and me, it was old-home week complete with dazzling sunlight everyday! We'd get loaded and take extended walks in the desert to puzzle it all out. For Tumor, it was his first trip to America's Southwest, and he was understandably a little rocked by the sensory overload of it all.

The way back was punctuated by a short stopover on Poland Ave, Modesto, CA, World Headquarters of the Universal Life Church, say Hallelujah! Kirby J. Hensley, the Exalted Poobah and Chief Potentate of Operations, espoused no particular doctrines, required no pledge of fealty, and furthermore, exacted no fee, though seemed grateful for our meager free-will offering. The honorable Reverend Hensley would simply issue an ordination certificate to anyone who asked for one.

What a concept! Define your own religious practice; define your own God! Now, that was our kind of religion, one that did not require special "credentials" in order to assume authority for personal belief, relevance of "God(s)," moral practice, purpose in life, and the like. Moreover, this formal, symbolic recognition and expropriation of power from entrenched authority—established religion—served as an example of the Hippie Code: Take control of your life!

This man must have struck a chord with folks. My certificate, dated February 13, 1969, is numbered 19,166; Chanren's and Tom's were no more than two digits away from mine. In the years to come, he and the Universal Life Church went on to issue over 18 million ordination certificates. Now, that's Freedom of Religion! Soon after returning to Oregon, I registered my ministerial credentials with the state, for a $2.00 fee. Reverend Yowell Mebsanuri was licensed to perform life-affirming services for virtually any occasion—for a consideration, to be negotiated. I have officiated/presided over no less than five marriage ceremonies over the years, all thanks to the revolutionary theologian (perhaps just shy of Martin Luther), Kirby J. Hensley. All power to the people!

The only other episode worth adding to the account of the Fabulous Furry Freak Brothers' raid on the American Southwest was in continuing the drive north of San Francisco through Marin County and into California's respectable wine country—Napa, Sonoma, and Mendocino Counties. To be sure, in terms of volume, the "center" of California wine country was Modesto, World Headquarters of Ernesto and Julio Gallo's jug wine empire. Here, in the north country, we were encountering frequent enticements along the freeway to stop off for a free wine tasting. So naturally, out of the spirit of scientific inquiry, we researched the wares of several tasting rooms, capped by Italian-Swiss Colony, where the various wines kept coming until you couldn't stand upright or clutch a glass any longer. Presumably a tax write-off, the wine was complimentary to the customer. Of course the conspicuous downside was that the chauffeur needed to show a little restraint in order to deliver his passengers safely, further on down the road.

No doubt Tom benefited from Chanren's watchful eye because I was beyond scrutinizing other people's behavior. Fortunately Tumor was able to maneuver the vehicle; they poured my limp carcass into the back seat, and we were on our way, having narrowly avoided Scylla on our voyage home—or was it Charybdis: Free wine? Right this way! By pandering to our baser lusts of gluttony and intoxication, these alcohol merchants seduced us. However, I hasten to admit, we willingly waded right in, eagerly fulfilling our role as the swine of the Homeric tale.

So there he is, Yowell, several sheets too many in a full gale, unable to sleep, restless and bored with interpreting the desultory grunts that pass for earnest colloquy in the front seats. He rummages around looking for something to distract him when an idle search under the driver's seat fetched a heavy, machined-steel implement… A GIANT FUCKING HANDGUN!! To be specific, a WWII vintage Army-issue Colt 45 semi-automatic, Tom behind the wheel explains. He hadn't thought to mention it, but it turns out he always packs on long trips. By this time, Tumes reported that not only was the gun loaded but cocked as well, Yowie had become the center of everybody's frantic attention. Everyone had earnest, emphatic, cautionary messages to impart, all at once, zipping down the freeway 65~70 mph.

How could this be? Literally, cocked with the safety on, one fervently hoped. Existentially, how this could be—how this gun, in these hands, in this car, with these people, at this place, under these circumstances—would have to wait for a more contemplative time.

Still half-lit but now rushing on adrenaline, Yowell ceases waving this lethal weapon around, bowels liquefying at the realization he could easily have blown a big hole through his brother, or Tom, the chauffer, and killed them all. Or he could've shot another car on the freeway. Rather than trying to follow Tummy's agitated verbal instructions on how to uncock the weapon, Mebs carefully, gingerly put the gun on the floor of the car—to an immediate sense of relief all around. The pressure had been released from the balloon.

Maybe we had an agenda that I just can't remember currently, but it was understood the point of our odyssey was to escape the drizzle for a few weeks with some amiable friends in the Sunny Southwest, nothing more. I bring this up because the effect of our visit turned out to be an impressive recruitment drive. Did we paint too rosy an idyll when we spoke of the interpersonal workings of the Yellow Submarine? Probably. In any event, a few months later Dana and Ned were the first of this new wave of members. Except that Ned didn't last two weeks, whereas Dana was having the time of her life—enjoying some interpersonal freedom of expression for the first time in a long time.

Next came Double T and Gina, with basically the same story. 2T took their VW bus and bolted inside of ten days. Something about seeing their wives willingly traipse off with one or another of the house studs, while the local female fare wasn't exactly falling into the laps of either abandoned hubby. A tough situation, to be sure.

The Feenyx Tracers also succumbed to the lure of the Emerald Empire, arriving by late-summer. "On Stage" Dogless, the raconteur, and wife Samantha came for the same out-of-state tuition waiver for grad school that had attracted Pollo. Since they qualified for married student housing they were able to avoid getting sucked into the Yellow Sub vortex, except for occasional party weekends and ceremonies, at which they were welcome and enthusiastic participants. I recall, if dimly, a particularly decadent Thanksgiving Bacchanal to which they contributed significant conviviality.

William Blake made manifest in Jim Morrison

Can you picture what will be, so limitless and free
desperately in need of some stranger's hand
in a desperate land... lost in a romance, wilderness of pain
waiting for the gentle rain

The End, The Doors

I can see that I'm getting soft in my 28 years. Preferring sheets with my bedding. Because Jay, at fifteen, doesn't give a damn. See the shadow of our parents' values get recapitulated here. It is not intuitive or particularly comfortable (for parent or parented) for a group of "adults" to assume a rather sudden parental role to the three minor siblings of a couple of members of our thrown-together family—otherwise to be cast to already beleaguered shirt-tail relatives, or worse, the welfare system. I ask Jay to make the bed he sleeps in, and in so doing, I would make him into a reflection of me. And Gagutz, and Karisma, and Lukas, in my image.

We all need someone you can lean on, and if you want to, you can lean on me...

You can't always get what you want, but if you try sometime, you just might find you get what you need.

Let it bleed, Can't always get..., Rolling Stones

"You create the needs to fulfill: you fulfill the needs you create." Sounds like a bullshit statement some tapped-out hippie might make.

If now isn't, in waiting is. The trick is to make it now, for now is timeless. There is no age. Marshall McLuhan and Tim Leary taught us (and more accurately Augustus Owsley Stanley III, who pharmacologically, psychotrophically empowered us to teach ourselves), the 5th dimension is inward—trans-spatially/trans-temporally. If you're there you don't have to go anywhere physically. The journey's in our head. Are you trippin', man?

We'll hold hands and watch the sunrise from the bottom of the sea.
But first, are you experienced? Not necessarily stoned but...
beautiful

Are You Experienced, Jimi Hendrix

This night Gina reminds me how important she is to me—and how prone I am to taking our relationship for granted. Tonight I'm missing her company but she is not missing mine; she's exchanging body fluids with Gristle, that opportunist weasel... I swear, turn your back for just a couple hours, there'll be some horny devil moving in on your operation...

Needless to say, there's more than a little tongue-in-cheek in the preceding paragraph. There is nothing about this operation that is remotely mine. I'm just reverting to a knee-jerk male chauvinism of possessiveness; I'm grousing because I find myself on the receiving end of what I preach: People—of either gender—are free to choose their (sexual) partners.

Hermano Chanren, where are you now on your Sadhana? Panama? Or yet Peru?

(from a journal entry, November 1969)

The US Census Bureau Encounters the Yellow Submarine

Around mid-April 1970, we had a strange visit. An Enumerator from the US Census Bureau, Commerce Department, came calling. It turns out we had failed to fill out and return in the self-addressed, postage-paid envelope our Constitutionally mandated Census report. I remember having looked over said form in conjunction with Tom, who dearly loved fucking with bureaucracy. Quarrel, even more so, and both of these gentlemen were at hand on the auspicious occasion of the visit. The form required several assumptions that were applicable in a normal household but not to ours. To wit, we were supposed to identify not only names and ages of every household member, but the relationship of everybody to everybody else. It was understood they had something else in mind than *Crewmate*. In the cases of Pollo and Gagutz, Chanren/Anita and Karisma, and even Chanren and me, we could identify parent(s) and children, and siblings easily enough. But what about the rest of us?

We basically were unable to get beyond the notion of Head of household. In Census-speak, that meant the one who paid the rent, the person in charge of/responsible for the occupancy of the dwelling in question. I can assure the reader the mere suggestion of someone in charge of our "household," the redoubtable Yellow Submarine, would have instantly raised hackles on any number of occupant/members. We were all Captains or there were no Captains; we are all Gods or there are no Gods. We paid homage to no "leader," for better or worse. The figurative, slang meaning of head as "a stoner, one who gets high," was not lost on us, either. In an egalitarian sense, we were virtually all heads in our house.

The worthy dictum, We are all responsible, did not hold particularly true in the daily practice of interpersonal behavior, but we Submariners closed ranks and presented a united front when it came to confrontations with agents of the Leviathan. None of us presumed the Census Bureau had any direct connection to military policy, or the Selective Service System, or the Vietnam War, but the Commerce Department's hands were doubtless bloody via any number of its involvements/machinations.

When it came down to it, we were simply ill disposed to aid Big Brother in any way. We were polite but emphatic; we would not cooperate. I'm afraid the Enumerator whelp had to limp away, tail tucked between his legs, having been intellectually savaged for his legitimate effort.

Confirming/Debunking Myths

When people think of hippie communes their minds are apt to lead them into descending loops of a Dantean Inferno—to lurid accounts of prurient, drug-induced orgies with Janis wailing "Ball and Chain" at crystal-shattering decibels. Are those rhythmic moans coming from the stereo or from the bedroom? Or that other darkened den? Black light reflected off phosphorescent paint smeared on select anatomical locations, pulsating to the music. A haze of pungent reefer smoke suspended throughout the house. Hot candle wax being dripped on quivering nipples—Anthony Comstock writhing in his grave! My, wasn't it exquisite being a life-form that reproduces sexually, and, while not that anxious to make babies just yet, having the opportunity to practice so often. Being young and pulsing with hormones in a permissive age.

> *Before you slip into unconsciousness I'd like to have another kiss,*
> *another flashing chance at bliss, another kiss.*
> *The crystal ship is being filled, a thousand girls, a thousand thrills*
> *a million ways to spend your time…*
>
> *The Crystal Ship,* The Doors

I must admit I had so hoped to chastise you, the naughty reader, for conjuring such depraved fantasies. But of course it's all true! Well, maybe not the fuckandsuck freeforalls, but between/among consenting adults, virtually every other possible combination… no wait! We did have some restrictions:

1. No Bestiality—of either inter-species possibility, if you catch my drift;

2. No Necrophilia, though frankly, we never had anyone croak on us to test this latter item; and

3. No Pedophilia. Alas, the record shows we failed in at least one example, and not just by one year—17 instead of 18, the Age of Consent in Oregon. In all likelihood, Candy Button was introduced to sexuality at thirteen years of age by Elvis Boinker, himself a good-looking cocksman of 18 or 19.

I'd have to say we had an unwritten fourth proscription: No hard drugs. No smack, no speed, morphine, none of those pharmaceuticals that were injected. No shooting up anything, period. This one was getting tossed by the time I left.

A prime example of our being sexually promiscuous, licentious, libertine and "open" was our STD epidemic, in the summer of 1969, otherwise known as the Summer of Rut.

Realms of bliss, realms of light, some are born to sweet delight.
Some are born to sweet delight. Some are born to the Endless Night,
They'll never learn, they'll never learn...

Move real slow; you like it more and more.
Take it as it comes; specialize in havin' fun

End of the Night, Take it as it Comes, The Doors

The upshot of it was eight or so of us developed symptoms (burning sensation in the nether regions, difficulty during micturition) within 3~4 days of the first person's symptoms, diagnosis, and beginning of treatment. As in her case, a bunch of us trundled down to White Bird Clinic, which summarily had us expose a haunch and take a wad of antibiotics, and a follow up oral regimen—but I'm a little hazy on that point.

Those White Bird folks must've gotten some fat grant buckos because we were basically among the urban indigent—you could say we were generally among the indignant indigent, but on this occasion grateful—and thus qualified for full treatment free. Hell, they thanked us for coming in and getting it taken care of, no doubt having some inkling of what a disease-incubation-and-transmission nexus the Yellow Submarine had the potential to be.

Tumor and I toyed with a sociogram of the disease-contact vectors. On a sheet of paper, we made a large ring of nine or ten small circles, one for each person infected. We assigned a letter to each person, and affixed one to each small circle. An arrowed line from G to D, for example, dated, would tell the reader that person G had infected person D. The date, if known, would help track the progress of the disease over time. Needless to say, in our mélange it was sometimes difficult to determine who introduced the infection to whom. In at least one case an individual seemed to have contracted the disease from more than one source within a 24-hour period—would that be a case of the wages of sin? True, the stats got a little murky by the time 8 or 9 people were infected.

Several people, I suspect, will breathe easier to learn these particular records are no longer extant. That crude "sociogram" was a back-of-an-envelope kind of record and probably didn't survive the week.

I don't think it was the clap—it must have been Chlamydia, or something like it. This was long before HIV/AIDS, and syphilis was practically unheard of in Eugene, our well-born muddy swale of a city. White Bird didn't even run cultures on us, if memory serves; just dosed us all based on the first person's examination, and sent us packing. After a week or 10 days of antibiotics in one form or another, we were back to our various strategies and ploys for getting laid, but with mutual admonitions to be more selective of the people we slept with outside the family.

Ha! Good luck with that one! This was 1969, two years post-Haight-Ashbury and that Summer of Love. This was Eugene, Oregon, the current Hippie Capital of the World. We may have been drug-addled and feckless, but virtually everybody between the ages of 16 and 36 was copulating like rabbits at the slightest provocation. Oh God, because we could! The spontaneity of it was magical. I recall getting better acquainted with a new friend on a summer's eve in the graveyard out behind the old Mac Court, and I can't imagine we were the first to desecrate the local dead in a frenzy of hormonally driven lust. Building rapport while probing her deeply on a matter of great, immediate concern, alas, long since forgotten.

* * * * *

*There's no time to lose I heard her say
Catch your dreams before they slip away
Dying all the time, lose your dreams
and you will lose your mind, a life unkind...*

Ruby Tuesday, Rolling Stones

The New World

If you wanted to hang out in a place that didn't serve booze, implying a quieter, gentler atmosphere than your typical copping-an-alcohol-buzz, boisterous-pub vibe, in those early days there was only one, the New World Coffee House. Located just a couple blocks out the campus main gate and around the corner from the original Maxie's Tavern, the owner and Maitre Dame, Alison Cadbury, had done it right. She offered the basic run of coffee drinks, cocoa, teas, Italian sodas, and an array of cookie/brownie/pastries that she or her staff baked, often on site. She also offered a choice of two house-made soups, and your standard selection of sandwiches, and salads.

The New World must have occupied half of an older house; it felt rather narrow with a solid internal wall running down the left side from the front, windows all on the right. Funny, I can't remember what might have been on the other side of that wall. Too much psycho-socially was always going on in the New World. Phonograph records (that's right, try to grasp before

I-Pods, before CDs came tape cassettes, before cassettes and 8-track, it was all vinyl or acetate records) were always playing, with the early focus on baroque/classical or jazz. Always something to complement polite, often measured and thoughtful conversation. Something soothing.

Functional tables and chairs, area lighting, a rotation of sometimes-provocative artists' paintings (ants crawling to/from a seated nude's vagina, that sort of thing) occupied the walls for months at a time. Spatially, aurally, visually, and often ofactorily, the scene was an altogether pleasant, affectively agreeable haven from the rain. Not so big as to feel cavernous, not so small as to feel crowded with 18~20 people, chillin' with the Eugene cognoscenti. Though no one was remotely conscious of it at the time, the New World Coffee House must have had good feng shui.

I can't recall who got hired first, Chanren? Gina? Someone else? I worked there for a while too. The Sub's first attempts at commercial production of Granola began, thanks to Alison, in the New World kitchen after the coffee house had shut down daily operations and cleaned up. It probably wasn't more than a few nights, and those test batches were 20 or 25 lbs. instead of the 50 to 60 lbs. we were making a night at our peak, but we figured out basic proportions, temperature, and baking time, before setting up our own licensed, commercial operation in the downstairs laundry room of the Sub, in the very bowels, as it were. But that New World kitchen was a classy place to do large-scale cooking: perfect lighting, a great sound system, and every food-preparation device you could possibly need at your fingertips—and several that were thoroughly mystifying, suggesting "marital aides," or body cavity surgery, as much as means to improve one's culinary repertoire.

I think all us Sub members who worked for Alison learned to be competent employees, and to be sure, there was a lot to get good at. Alas, not more than three months into my career as barista/general help I was canned without explanation. Which smarted a good deal, especially since I really couldn't think of a policy I'd breached, a slight I'd committed, a faux pas I'd lurched into... Well, there was this one lee-e-etle habit I had fallen prey to on my shift.

The Submariners certainly didn't usher in the change in musical selection featured at the New World, but we probably accentuated the tendency. From very tasteful Vivaldi or J S Bach, perhaps Miles, or the MJQ, the platters flipped to the likes of Dr. John, Tiny Tim, and the Troggs. It happened quick; the old timers must have thought they'd lost their grip on reality. The siege was broken, the walls had been breached, the Vandals were at hand, and they weren't taking male prisoners. After all, we were in the throes of the Second Tsunami of Rock'n'Roll; there were simply too many amazing musical expressions exploding on the scene not to play as many of them as often as possible. Nonetheless, it was understood that our musical choices were supposed to approximate the, dare I say, understated ambiance of the New World.

Once in a while, though, when the right song was playing—say, the Who's Don't get fooled again, or the Doors' When the music's over—I would sooth the customers, much in the manner of Hayden in his "Surprise" Symphony, lull them with a diminished, subdued volume, only to crank it up to just shy of the speaker-rending level at the precise moment Roger Daltry, or "Lizard King" Morrison, delivered his monumental shriek.

The effect was stunned silence, even briefly after the volume was returned to a sedate level; for those three or four seconds the vocalist had our complete attention. After which, normalcy and order proceeded as if nothing had happened. Ah, but, since that insignificant little prank occurred a handful of times, it's possible Alison got wind of it and chose to nip the insurrection in the bud. Dispose of the bad apple, as it were. Get a fresh start with more tractable help.

Despite this, ahem, minor personal issue, until Bill and Cindy Wooten opened the Odyssey downtown on Willamette St. in the fall(?) of '69, there was no other remotely equivalent public venue in Eugene to the New World Coffee House. Aside from being prime trolling grounds, it was a true sanctuary.

A word about my seduction skills: I was never a body-builder/strut-my-physique kind of guy. I grew up "four eyes" through years when wearing glasses was rare enough—from first grade on—to warrant frequent ridicule from my peers. Also, I waged a fierce battle with acne during adolescence, reinforcing my marginalization and introversion. Being hamburger-faced was clearly not prime ass-bandit material. To be sure, everyone has her/his own less-than-desirable traits. For better or worse, (some of?) mine were available for public review and subsequent critique early on. While others manage to sail through high school, even college, with unsavory, weasely characteristics undetected—the jocks are a stereotypical example—only to have the insidious worm of selfishness, annoyance and alienation emerge later in life.

From such psychologically fragile beginnings I cultivated humility, patience, and subtlety. Many would argue I failed miserably in the humility department, and subtlety seems to have morphed into something more sinister, something akin to deviousness, or cunning. As for patience, who's got the time?

In any event, without overtly making a move on a woman, without pressing my desire, but showing restraint, building interests in common, building rapport over the course of an evening, I was able to pick up (was picked up by? How do we determine these things?) a willing young woman on at least one occasion while on duty at the New World. This is not braggadocio so much as an indication of how relaxed the sex mores were in those pre-HIV/AIDS days. Lothario I wasn't, though my long, golden tresses didn't seem to hurt my chances any.

Hair

At one point by late '69 I figured I had the second longest hair in Eugene—after Del Pearl, a short kid whose dense, curly hair stood straight out from his head about two feet in all directions (I know, you're thinking, Gee Willikers, Yowie, that sure is quite the Claim to Fame!). Long hair on a man was one of the easiest, most conspicuous ways to draw a contrast between oneself and the mainstream society. The manly men's response to a guy's long hair was to let you know in various ways you were not masculine, were outright effeminate, and very probably homosexual.

I usually wore my hair loose, which made the motion of my hair—through sudden swing or shake of my head—a not-sexual, but very sensual experience. Far from making me perceived as less masculine/more effeminate than burr heads, I'd say unequivocally, long hair contributed to getting me laid far more than short hair ever did. I actually had an attractive young woman once approach me out of the blue, run her hand down the back of my long, dirty-blond hair, and say, I wish my hair were as beautiful as yours. I see no reason to be embarrassed enjoying the sensations associated with hair that for generations, off and on, were common only to women.

The freak flag may have served primarily as a kind of litmus. The women who considered long hair on a man an offence would signal "Warning! Stay away!" before you even got close. In the other hand, those damsels not intimidated by your golden tresses might let you get closer still... Like the young ladies that make themselves available to rock musicians and NBA players, some women have been curious enough to want to count coup on a hippie.

Inasmuch as hair grows through the dermis from pockets containing nerve endings, it is quite obviously an extension of the skin. One feels through the hair, only more softly, more subtly than through direct contact with the skin. Obvious though it may be, this is a realization I'd never made prior to the time my head hair had grown long enough to hang some inches from my body, helping me extend the sensation of head motion, and anticipate objects it comes in contact with, like a cat's whiskers. Modest by some standards, my tresses have become my chief vanity, my number one affectation. Physically, it gets in my way sometimes, and it's harder to keep clean than shorter styles to be sure, but it's worth it. Long hair suits my identity these months/years. Certainly a niggling thing to come between me and another with differing tastes, one would think.

Or is it? I've been fond of rationalizing that there is no justifiable criticism, no valid defense, for the matter of personal aesthetics; one could choose to adorn or not to adorn oneself in any fashion short of directly infringing on other beings…No, friend, the apoplexy you suffer at the sight of my golden locks, radiant in the sunlight… That's your karma, not mine. Still, when untold thousands of America's youth—virtually all the people I choose to associate with—spontaneously forsake Gillette and the local barber, one wonders about the spontaneous collaboration of teens-and-twenties—pre computer/pre-cell phone, let alone Twitter/Facebook—everywhere, even internationally, how to explain it if not as out-right conspiracy?

It was possible to see in this behavior, an element of theater. We were trying out roles of our own choosing. The mask, the new persona, was useful in establishing a counter-culture stance against the mainstream American narrative (explicitly Imperialist/Capitalist expansion abroad, consumerism/regimentation/dehumanization at home), and our clothing choices were apt to mock haute couture. Damn straight, I'm rebelling against society! I will wear my hair long at least until I no longer hear:

Hey faggot! or,
Is it a boy or a girl? or,
If you'd shave, I'd marry you.

Or just a wolf whistle. Speaks volumes about their own sexual insecurities, wouldn't you say? So every time some middle-aged, atrophied, pompous, sneering SOB passes me, I nod, smile, and say,

Yeah, uh huh, that's right, I'm doin' it.
No time out, no king's ex; not next week, not next year.
Right here and now, today, living my life as I want it.
No alarm clocks (no clocks!), no schedules, no bosses, no uniforms,
Just me living my life as fully as I know how.
Doin' it, you miserable honky, jes' doin' it.

For a long time I thought the pose was credible in that so many of us believed, for a while at least, we were going to change the way things were done; we would make a difference. We were going to change the fucking world, man!

The Three Stooges encounter Three Graces

A city-wide, all-day party was scheduled for one late spring Saturday. I don't recall the pretext for this outdoor picnic event, End of school, Summer Solstice, Fourth of July? It would be a full year before the first Earth Day would happen, but whatever the occasion, this shindig was held in Skinner Butte Park along the river, with the hill as a backdrop. A delegation of Submariners was enlisted to the task of attending the event, maintaining the requisite decorum as officers and representatives of the Submarine, while making appropriate contact with members of the community.

Among the volunteers for this arduous detail were Chanren, Tom, and I, freshly returned from our foray into the Southwest—though, there was serious divergence of interpretation as to the manner and appropriateness of contact with community members the various parties had in mind—sailors on shore leave, and all that.

There was live music non-stop; since it was all outdoors, you could move up close or wander off to suit yourself, depending on your affliction/affiliation to the group performing and your willingness to court permanent hearing loss. Other distractions included the spontaneous parade, for example. People decked out in hip-rageous attire, frisbees describing graceful aerodynamic arcs, soap bubbles wafting on the breeze, along with the pungent aroma of burning ganja—it all made for an idyllic public event. To tell the truth, it felt like we were collectively basking in our newfound solidarity in Freakdom. Struttin' our stuff, as it were. Lettin' it all hang out. Fer sher.

Taking a break from the too-close, too-loud music scene, our three gallants were strolling along the river when they chanced upon three comely lasses, three puppies in tow. After the formalities of introduction, on hearing the swains were recently ordained ministers, legitimately able to perform any ceremony those big shots in those muckity-muck churches could perform—and a hell of a lot they *wouldn't,* wink, wink—our new-found friends quickly called our bluff. They had become quite fixated on the spectacle of having us baptize their goddamn dogs. They were so persuasive in their plaintive appeal that at least one of us was convinced he was going to get lucky as a consequence of this charade; Tumor was going to become Tumescent! Thus, of course, we wound up standing up to our ankles in the Willamette River, making up some heretical consecration of the waters and the sacredness of the occasion, then a quick dunk of puppies in the water (to assure their ascent into heaven?), and return them to their beaming Mamas.

I thought it was more than a little bizarre, but the maidens were sufficiently impressed to hang out with us, later to visit us at the commune, and ultimately two of the three—Katy and Molly—joined our ranks. Alas, the lithe and cat-like Rita slipped away (Lovely Rita, meter maid, come quick! Check my pulse; I think my heart is racing. I may require succor…).

The Dispossession of Earthly Goods

At one point Yowie must have been between fairly serious connections with the ladies—and the turf to fend for that seems to accompany them. In an inexplicable impulse he gave up all his worldly possessions to the Family. He was acting out what they'd collectively talked about all along. He was walking the talk. It was understood that, like Gandhi, he would keep his prescription glasses—not good for anyone else's eyes, his modest wristwatch, a toothbrush and his small pocketknife. Everything else, his records, books, artwork, clothes, shoes, hat, belt, meager stash of tools—everything became everyone's. He would live to regret this, but at the time he felt very purified and liberated. Light of foot, figuratively and literally.

Did anyone follow the inspiring example of His Yowness? Everything is everyone's would seem, after all, to be implied within the concept of communal living. It's a simple idea: The People's books go in the People's library where anyone can use them. Clothes get washed, dried, and sorted into bins according to male/female, shirts/ pants/socks/underwear in the People's clothes pantry for the People to use. And so on, through all general-use things. While the notion of private property was certainly a worthy topic for debate, so too, was the concept of privacy itself, at least to the extent it is assumed to be a birthright in modern society. Some other folks followed the example somewhat; it worked for a while.

(On reading this portion, Chanren offered this critique)
There are two words I would utter in response to your seeming-to-wonder why your/our temporary experiment in communal property didn't work: Sammy Costas. I don't know if you remember this character. He was an ex-boyfriend of Lark's who sometimes came around and

was a serious kleptomaniac. Or else he was feeding a habit...

Ultimately, most folks, given the choice, don't easily give up private space and their attendant private things. The pressure on coupled relationships is perhaps too great to permit surrendering private space/private things. It must be the fabled nesting impulse, the urge to personalize a space in subconscious preparation for creating a family, or something like it. And while we did get beyond pair bonding some of the time for some people, in the end the lure to form more-or-less stable, exclusive couples was always a major dynamic, some might say anchor, of the Yellow Submarine.

Pets

When it's non-stop people twenty-four/seven, it doesn't have to be a swarming mass of hippies to qualify as an exhausting level of interpersonal contact. You might think such a crew as the Yellow Submarine would forego the need for a pet—and you'd be thinking right. Malcolm and Mudra's pair of malamute-huskies weren't really sociable, but they came as a package back when we were only ten or eleven members. They weren't threatening so much as eternally wary, suspicious, even a little surly. And of course, big. When the time came, I wasn't sorry to see them go. Frankly, anything but a friendly, extremely well socialized, mid-sized dog would have had difficulty surviving the vicissitudes of life aboard the Sub.

Any self-respecting cat, even a hungry one, would've sized up the prospects early on, which is to say nine excruciating lives with an indeterminate number of these big, noisy, klutzy creatures, a contingency of whom seems to operate around the clock making incredibly loud electronic noises—and taken the dignified way out: wandered into the street at the strategic moment.

We had no turtles, no goldfish, no exotic snakes, though for a while we did keep a rabbit. Circumstances of acquisition are murky, but let's posit a plausible scenario with Jay as protagonist. Probably in conjunction with Candy or Mud, Jay came across this abandoned child's pet on a romp through the park. The novelty of this living, cuddly bunny had worn thin since Easter, while the necessary care continued day in, day out:

What to do? I know; little bunny's all grown up now. Let's take him up to the park where he'll have lot's of grass to eat, and he'll be happy... Well, it was a good(?) thing one of our tribe discovered Br'er Rabbit before the first off-leash dog of any size came along, because in such an event, li'l thumper would've come to a quick and brutal end.

Needless to say, one doesn't toilet train a rabbit, any more than one teaches a guppy the ABCs, but unlike most other farm animals, rabbits have the decency to aggregate their fecal deposits into odorless (once dried) oblong pellets easy to scoop up and toss out the window of the attic dormitory where Jay and mostly the bachelors slept. Of course, the solid waste was only half the problem, but somehow we managed to delude ourselves as to that other function, the liquid excrescence—for a while at least.

In the summer, with decent weather, people would climb out that south-facing window onto a large deck and sunbathe, or otherwise lounge with a joint and a boombox. Rabbit, our black, young-adult rabbit—gender unknown—often accompanied us out onto that slightly sloping deck, and could be trusted to stay out there unattended, with food and water nearby. With a brain too small to be programmed for large drop offs, Rabbit never fell off the edge, as far as we know.

Truth to tell, I don't know what happened to Rabbit, our companion of six or eight weeks. We don't even know if he'd been left out on the roof, where he couldn't leave on his own, and was potentially prey to a hawk flying by. Otherwise, there was no good explanation. He'd never descended the stairs from the dorm to the kitchen before; I don't think he could have anatomically managed the feat in one piece. Furthermore, no Yellow Sub meal was forthcoming with anything resembling "chicken" as its animal protein source. I guess it's always possible that someone had discovered rabbit-urine-soaked bedding, or prized article of clothing, when no one else was around and, in the spirit of the moment, took matters into his/her own hands. Which is pure speculation, I freely admit.

Rabbit continued in Sub lore long past its corporal occupancy and mysterious disappearance, with us one day and gone the next in the grand scope of things. Couple this unexplained absence with the fact that we were chronically lax in cleaning our living quarters, as our story continues. Before people were ready to sleep and on other occasions, small groups often hunkered around the hearth—the record player—somebody rolling a joint, another person doubtless selecting the music, somebody else perhaps crumbling hash into a pipe. This hadn't risen to the level of a nightly ritual primarily because people went to bed—to sleep—at different times. The space was first, a dormitory, secondarily, play space.

On one of the two occasions my parents visited us, my father, several other commies, and I spent some laid back time together sitting around cross-legged in that very location, listening to Workingman's Dead and toking up. Dad reported later that he could see how people might enjoy the ol' killer weed—and the Grateful Dead wasn't half-bad, either!

He claimed that experience had been his "maiden voyage" with Maria Juana, which I found a little hard to believe. He grew up in Douglas, AZ, a small town literally on the Mexican border, so I always assumed he'd had plenty of opportunities for youthful indiscretions, including smoking the noble weed. (My own maiden voyage was with kiff, a powdery hash, in the medina in Casablanca, Morocco, just shy of my 21st birthday—another story.)

Commune lore speaks of somesuch group as ours trying desperately to get high, hyperventilating to no avail on some fairly harsh shit: *Hey, I just found this chunk of hash I lost yesterday! It must've fallen between these cushions. Where's that hash pipe?*

To date, no evidence, anecdotal or otherwise, has been brought forward asserting euphoric or hallucinogenic effects from smoking desiccated rabbit turds.

The Yellow Sub Repels Grosse Pointe Assault

After three months of living with us Molly Snow—our only heiress—finally broke down and wrote her grandparents, her legal guardians, that she was living in a commune. She should have told them long before because they were getting mixed messages, garbled versions, from various sources, which only fed their anxiety. Just as there was nothing for Molly to do in the end but come clean with her grandparents, there was nothing for them to do but fly in from Grosse Pointe bastions of monopolistic, usurious, "free-market" capitalism, to Eugene, Oregon—wellborn, well-meaning, if somewhat naïve, fading-woodman's town—to conduct the battle from the field. So it was on that sunny morning with the cab driving uncertainly nearer, finally asking directions from our neighbor, the old scion peering out from the back seat, hostility somehow a compensation for failing eyesight. Those who were up could feel the vibes, knew it was them and called all compos mentis hands to their battle stations.

Into the house without a knock, *Where is Molly, please?*

Given the hour, she's probably asleep. Would you care to sit down while I go wake her?

That won't be necessary, just point out the room. With proprietary gall, the patrician grandparents marched into their heiress granddaughter's room, said young woman being fortunately asleep—by herself! (A collective sigh of relief)

Gina passed some awkward moments with them while Molly dressed.

How many people live here?

About fourteen currently.

How many bathrooms have you, then?

Two.

Oh, my heavens, how do you stand it? Then, away for breakfast and... The Meeting. Away somewhere for the Conference, in a neutral setting where the communal bias might not be so strongly felt.

Will you come back to Detroit with us now? All this is putting a terrible strain on your grandmother... Comes the intimidation less subtle: If you don't come back with us, we shall have to begin an investigation of that house and all the pimps, whores, and dope fiends who live there.

Two of the charges were laughably off the mark: In no sense was sexuality being marketed for financial gain. When everyone is an amateur—literally engaged in the act for the love of it—there is no room for the pros. Clearly, no one's sexuality was being managed by someone else for profit. No prostitutes meant no pimps.

Ah, but that third item could be problematic, depending on how closely one might want to slice dope fiend...

After five hours of that barrage a limp Molly, eyes glazed, came back to us. Should she just return with them peaceably and be done with it? They had let slip what was in store for her, mentioning the need for her to be observed "briefly" in a Detroit psychiatric facility—any girl brought up the way she had been, who saw fit to live in such squalid conditions, was clearly in need of psychiatric evaluation.

We fell silent, awe struck, as we contemplated the wrath our moneyed antagonists could muster. Some of the laws we might have been vulnerable to included lewd cohabitation and contributing to the delinquency of minors. We violated zoning restrictions by allowing more than five people to live together, unrelated by blood or marriage. On this latter issue, we'd undergone two investigations, narrowly out-weaseling officialdom the second time. And of course the specter of a drug bust loomed always near. Everyone had heard of the Man "discovering" evidence, even when the house was clean—which ours wasn't. Molly had emphasized our household non-use of illegal drugs, probably overstating her case as she did so. Who could fathom what a zealous District Attorney with a strong mandate might come up with pouring over the minutia of an established hippie hangout?

Granola, our chief source of income, was eminently bustable. Our "commercial kitchen" was a joke. The prospects were almost unlimited when you tried to conceive of us Submariners from the eyes of the straight world, titillated by our flaunting of the sexual taboos. Weren't we adulterers, statutory rapists? Polygamists? From there, it's a small step to Sodomites and bestiaphiles. To say nothing of harborers (and thereby, accessories) of runaways.

The idea of the grandparents pursuing a sanity hearing in hopes of finding Molly incompetent and unable to manage her trust fund, followed by having her placed near at hand under their watchful scrutiny, led us to think all we could do was stash the smokin' rope and prepare for the siege.

The next morning, however, at the Rendezvous for Her Decision, these vindictive geriatrics with old money and blue-blood clout said they'd consulted their lawyer, and had reluctantly been persuaded to allow her to stay. Must have been a shrewd lawyer to perceive that Molly, who, as an adult, chose to live in this commune. She was perhaps not as demonstrably crazy as they thought she was.

Truth to tell, by this time several of us were virtually salivating at the possibility of access to an official, public venue—such guerilla theater as a courtroom would present could be really exciting—to be able to explore the notion of sanity, Molly's as well as our collective sanity, vis-à-vis a whole range of social "norms" going woefully under-examined by our co-opted Fourth Estate. The pulse quickens at the thought.

> *Sing we for love and idleness,*
> *Naught else is worth the having.*
> *Though I have been in many a land,*
> *There is naught else in living.*
> *And I would rather have my sweet,*
> *Though rose-leaves die of grieving,*
> *Than do high deeds in Hungary*
> *To pass all men's believing.*
>
> *An Immorality,* Ezra Pound

Fire!

Late summer, 1969, we had our fire. It was during those halcyon days when the family was its biggest with some 25 people in two houses—having communized our neighbors, the Thompsons—and we were perhaps least possessive in terms of space and relationships.

It was before the rains had kicked in and we were half way through tying the main-house sewer line into the city main. The city had annexed our neighborhood the year before, and had installed a sewage main straight down the middle of the only access to the Yellow Sub Annex/Thompson household, and the Orums, our neighbors directly down the hill from the main house. We'd gotten the landlord, a kindly soul, to let us dig the trench and lay the pipe, paying us a "princely" $2/person-hour while understandably taking longer, instead of contracting the job out to a commercial outfit, costing him many times the amount per hour, but having it done inside of 48 hours.

Pollo, putatively in charge of the operation, in spite Quarrel's persistent, contentious intervention, understood we were obliged to inform the city fire marshal of our intent (actually, seek permission) to tear up the only access road to two homes. Alas, el Pollito Estimable had somehow overlooked that requirement. Something about "finishing that part of the hookup in a day or two…minimize bureaucratic hassle…" So here we were approaching the end of our second week of having a 8-foot diameter, 5-foot deep bomb crater in the center of our common driveway, and a trench, like the front at Verdun in "The war to end all wars," running to the house.

On the evening in question Gina and I were down at the lower house in front of the fireplace, Gagutz crashed on a bed alongside a wall, when Pollo came in to see where his wayward son had gotten to. Seeing us settled in before a dwindling fire, and not wanting to wake the waif up, or, worse yet, pack his deeply asleep carcass up to the mother ship, El Pollito decided to leave him there for the night. That should have been all right; Gagutz, at 6, knew the lay of the land and was comfortable around fellow Submariners/friends. But someone had left the thermostat notched, I don't know, maybe in the high 60s. Soon after Pollo left, we damped down our all-but-dead fireplace blaze and retired to her boudoir for more private pursuits.

The next thing I know, out of a deep sleep someone is shouting, Get up quick! The livingroom's on fire! Gagutz's bed had been pushed up against the wall; the mattress skirting hung directly onto the electric baseboard heater, which the thermostat activated as the evening got cooler. That nasty acrylic material smoked and smoldered and finally got the wall and mattress hot enough to burn in earnest. As I recall, after safeguarding the human inhabitants, it took 4 or 5 adults maybe 15 minutes to get the fire under control, what with the garden hose from an outdoor spigot and pots of water drawn from the kitchen sink. Which was the approximate time it took for the fire department to show up.

It was a good damn thing we had the fire all-but out since the pros with their fancy gear were simply not going to be driving within 50 yards of the site of the fire that night, a fact that conspicuously perturbed them. We were fortunate we didn't lose Gagutz or anyone else to smoke inhalation, and on the next order of magnitude, the house and contents. I don't recall any really dire consequences befalling us for tying up a public access—I don't think we paid a fine—except thereafter we did complete the sewage line hookup with amazing alacrity.

Rivendale

By the fall of 1969, a full year after its inception, the commune had undergone changes, personnel fluctuations being chief among them. Between mid-June with the arrival of Geary, followed in mid-July by Quarrel and Doris Stockton and son Luke, to Elvis's arrival in mid-September, there were 18 newcomers. Many of those didn't stay long; others, such as Chanren and recent arrival, Terra, and Pollo and son Gagutz, left by the end of January. There was a mix, a froth of new power alliances and new ideas as to how we should be. One of the notions that became generally agreeable to everyone was to incorporate ourselves with the state as a non-profit, limited-liability corporation (LLC).

It was a bit of an exercise of placing the cart before the horse, but the intent was to position ourselves to be a legal, collective entity toward the purchase of rural land. In that sense it was worth doing, I guess, but the thing was, having incorporation papers didn't make us one whit more solvent. Our vaunted documents and a cashier's check for $100,000 would've gotten us in the door on some real estate opportunities. Whereas, papers or no papers, we couldn't have mustered $10,000 among the lot of us. Absent a wildly improbable pot of gold, rural land purchase was not going to be in our immediate future.

That heady fervor of legal recognition was part of assuming responsibility for who we were—part of that hippie ethos—and many people at the time argued for signaling our renewal, if you will, by adopting a new name to go along with this new status. The matter was considered and eventually passed in somesort of a poll. Rivendale became our legal name, and for a while folks actively promoted the change, though old habits die hard. Plus, a lot of folks didn't wholly buy the rationale for the name change. With hardly a ripple of public acknowledgement, Yellow Submarine remained our familiar moniker. The abstraction of a new legal name didn't turn out to change anything.

During that resurgence, though, we were interviewed by some folks from the local rag, The Augur. I don't remember the interview or the journalists' visit but I suspect it must've occurred in February or March of 1970, during a phase when we were sufficiently full of optimism and promise—to go along with the hormones—to present a strong picture of unity of intent. I think this comes through despite several prominent errors in the article otherwise.

The Mother Earth News, a new publication that year, picked up that original article and ran it in their July-August 1970 edition. The following, then, is a reprint of a reprint. We thank Brandy Ernzen of The Mother Earth News for permission to reprint the article in its entirety.

<u>Rivendale</u>
<u>About Rivendale and how the commune spirit continues near Eugene, Oregon.</u>
<u>By Dave Johnson and Aragorn</u>
<u>July/August 1970</u>

Originally published in the Eugene, Oregon Augur. Rivendale is a commune of 20 adults, five children, two dogs, too many cats and a pony living on four acres close to Eugene, Oregon.

Named for a mythical elf city in Tolkien's Middle Earth, the commune was started in August, 1968 by "Pip" Cole and John Butler. The primary goal of Rivendale is to provide a large family unit in which all members work for a common good. The secondary goal is a move toward self-sufficiency. Although some members have a strong desire to be relatively independent of the consumer society, others are less concerned with disaffiliation. Many members work in Eugene and the commune buys much of its supplies.

But most of the food is grown in the community's two gardens. The meals consist of vegetables, nuts, fruits, rice and homemade bread. Little meat is eaten, but a strictly vegetarian diet is not stressed.

In theory, everyone is expected to work according to his ability. But the commune has learned that some people naturally "pull more weight" than others.

This and other day-to-day problems that exist in society have to be coped with at the commune. Because it is a microcosm, the community feels these problems more acutely.

When a hassle develops, a general meeting is called. The gathering centers around what Tony Cole calls a "dialogue". This is a talk session in which the problem is brought into the open and discussed by all members. An attempt is then made to get general approval of a solution. This dialogue form of problem solving is one of the commune's many experiments in group living.

Another experiment was a marathon in which members stayed in one room for three days. Led by an advisor from Senoi Institute, the family tried to communicate through all the senses.

The commune is not accepting applicants at this time. Members feel there is neither actual nor emotional room for new people. They are planning to move to a more rural area and, as an incorporated non-profit organization, they hope to purchase some land.

Due to exploitation by news media, Rivendale is leary of exposure and publicity. But its members also try to avoid an atmosphere of mystique. Recently, they held an open house, inviting neighbors to come and ask questions about the commune.

Many members feel that Rivendale has developed a personality but the individuals who live there are a mixture of opposites. Some are actively involved in politics, others are apolitical, a few are into personal hangups and still others are concerned with society's problems. Their one common ground is Rivendale.

Doris, Quarrel and Luke Stockton

The Golden Age of Chemistry

Looking back, that period may have been the Golden Age of Chemistry, licit and otherwise. Birth control pills had hit their stride in the society at large. In one stroke women finally had reproductive control over their own bodies— Better living through chemistry! Virtually any sexually active female could get a prescription, and so pretty much all our women folk did. No houseful of babies (please!) in a family we were often not so sure about as it was.

But a consideration of the wonders of applied chemistry would be sorely incomplete without some modest commentary about ol' $C_{20}H_{25}N_3O$, lysergic acid di-ethylamide, a tool for a truly other-worldly experience. At least it was for me. As far as Intergalactic Space Cowboy status goes, I was naught but a Light, or maybe, Middle Weight. I've dropped acid maybe twelve, fifteen times. As for other hallucinogens, Mescaline and Psylocybin, maybe a half-dozen times each, but I never thought they could do the heavy psychic lifting that acid was capable of. Some of the trips were dazzling, transcendent experiences, others were a miserable, grit-your-teeth endurance of the 6 to 8 hour methamphetamine-wired rollacoaster ride some miscreant provider had supplied you instead of the pure, clear, zero-affect LSD promised.

That would not have happened with Clyde, a man who stood behind his product. Early on, we developed a mutually beneficial relationship with Clyde, a very sociable guy who liked to stimulate gatherings with some of his wares. He became our Saturday morning drop-in psycho-pharmacologist. You got your mail, your newspaper delivered to your door. We had our door-to-door, drop-in drug delivery, complete with cheerful explanations as to potencies, origins, unique features, and the cost/barter range for his wares. His satchel of goodies ran from pot to hash, to 'shrooms, to peyote, to acid, often top quality blotter acid. We'd chip in a few bucks for this or that, and he was always generous with free samples.

So we're sittin' around that big room off the kitchen, with that huge picture window looking south, up the valley, on a prototypical spring Saturday morn, into our second or third cup of coffee, joints being passed around. The most natural thing in the world would be to stick a ½-inch-square piece of blotter into one's tepid coffee, sipping it while enjoying the conversation and taking in the view.

Before you know it, the walls begin undulating, throbbing to the music and 12 or 13 people are psychic puddles on the floor. Said amorphous psychic clouds that inhabit recognizable forms have the ability to appear stunning, wondrous, and miraculous. Or hideous, repulsive, and thoroughly repugnant. Or anything in between, depending entirely on non-rational cues. Thus, we have a dozen heretofore recognizable, more-or-less rational folks with their psyches exploded to infinity by 11 o'clock in the morning! The expression, *Have a nice day*, takes on interesting dimensions under such circumstances. The idiom, *out of one's mind*, is quite literally accurate with the involvement of LSD.

> *I can see through mountains, watch them disappear,*
> *I can even touch the sky*
> *Swallowing the colors of the sounds I see,*
> *am I just a crazy guy? You bet!*
>
> *Flying high again,* Ozzie Osborne

Ah, but the things you can see! You become a sort of an open-ended sieve, and the you part disappears. So this physical entity that for 28 years or so housed what had been the style, the schtik, the recognizable characteristics, the outlook, and the personality of Yowell Mebsanuri, sees, hears, smells, feels, and otherwise perceives what Yowie could, plus some awareness (hypersensitivity?) beyond normal perception. But more importantly (and this is important!), this special ability to perceive is unencumbered by the knowledge, assumptions, expectations, or points of view of that former, familiar entity, his Yowness. Even though it's chemically induced, even though the duration is no more than 10 to 12 hours, to see/experience things completely afresh, no filters, no ego, I am here to tell you, can be truly wonderful, in its purist sense: full of wonder.

If the experience takes away the "you," perhaps that you is supplanted with all-being. Or the I-Thou, instead of the default position of I-It. And not to worry, that "you" that was so surely gone will be back, perhaps a little humbled, in a half-day or so. I didn't drop frequently, but remember I sometimes characterized the trip as therapeutic, a means of steam-cleaning your engine, defragging your computer, of sweeping the cobwebs from your attic, accumulating over the months/years.

Implicit in this is the understanding that the insights gained were to benefit the one who dropped when s/he returned to land of the Here & Now, when you return to your senses. Taking out the garbage and fixing the leaky faucet dare not be ignored for long. I never bought into the crypto-mystical hippie mythos that I might "get so high, I'll never come down…"

Disclaimer

Lest you, the reader, be laboring under a false impression, it goes without saying that one should never do drugs—or anything illegal, for that matter. Running afoul of the law is nobody's idea of a fun time (except perhaps for the lawyers, lingering in shallow waters, like leeches), certainly not the alleged perpetrator. Episodes in the narrative that appear to present wanton, debauched, flagrant drug taking in a favorable light are unintended and coincidental. Taken out of context, as it were.

As for tobacco, booze, caffeine, high-fructose corn syrup, and the multi-billion $ prescription drug industry, well, those drugs are just hunky dory, as anybody knows. You pays your money, and you takes your choice. Oh, and since cacao is still considered a legitimate product, keep your mitts off my Xocolatl, capish?

Let not young souls be smothered out before
They do quaint deeds and fully flaunt their pride.
It is the world's one crime its babes grow dull,
Its poor are ox-like, limp and leaden-eyed.
Not that they starve, but starve so dreamlessly;
Not that the sow, but that they seldom reap;
Not that they serve, but have no gods to serve;
Not that they die, but that they die like sheep.

The Leaden-eyed, Vachel Lindsay

The Story of Elvis Boinker

Elvis Boinker came to the Sub in September of 1969 on recommendation or request of Cleda, a long-time friend of early Sub occupants. Like Cleda, he was SoCal, in need of a new community. There were hints of legal scrapes—sometimes these things are better left unexamined. Ignorance can be, if not bliss, then plausible deniability. At 18 or 19 it wasn't clear whether Elvis had completed high school. To some extent what he may have lacked as a scholar he made up for on the football team, for a while anyway. What position he played is unknown; he was a strong, robust young man, so he could have played several positions—that is, until he took a tackle that crippled him thenceforth. Oh, he walks, though it was more like a hobble.

Yowell confessed to being a little leery about Elvis right off the bat. With thick, black hair, sideburns down to his jawbone, and an inscrutable smile, Yowie thought, If he's as cocky and full of himself as he looks, he's gonna be trouble. But to his credit, Elvis avoided policy debates, protocol discussions, and all such mental/verbal pyrotechnics that occupied the young Turks, their psychic sparring frequently on display.

Beyond being non-confrontational, Elvis seemed genuinely positive, upbeat, and friendly. He gave off no hostile vibes, so the males gradually took him to be non-threatening. Meanwhile, quite a few of the maidens found him attractive enough to set up shop with him for weeks, months sometimes.

When Yowie recently raised the issue of the impressive list of damsels Elvis had diverted during his occupancy, he demurred, perhaps signaling that the experience was not about with whom, and when, and for how long. Neither was it an achievement list, nor a mark of manhood. Here are his responses to the questions Yowell submitted:

What drew you to the Sub? What were your expectations at that point?

Different people from all over the United States. Community of people living together. Being self-sufficient and sharing ideas. Foxy ladies that love to play. Things were very good in the late sixties and early seventies; expectations were very high at the time. Lots of peace and love. Things have not changed; all the world needs is love, good day sunshine, rainy day woman to make it work.

How was your experience of the Sub different from your expectations?
My experience was very good, and enjoyed myself, met my expectations: New World Coffee House and Yellow Submarine Granola, distributing product to the Kesey crowd at the Springfield Creamery and food cooperatives, Nancy's Yogurt, still eat it today. Acid tests, expanding my outlook at life and the world I live in. Mother Earth was here before I was here and will be here after I'm gone. We need to take care of her for our children, grandchildren.

What pulled/pushed you away from the Sub?
Starting a new family, the need for privacy. I'm the same person I was then; I enjoy the same things that I enjoyed before. I hope that the world could take our ideas and realize we have only one planet to live on. Hope, compassion, some peace and harmony. Look for some personal enlightenment within ourselves that will radiate back to the rest of the world. I'm older and wiser from living life in the present, not the past, not trying to program the future. Live it day by day, moment by moment. Life's a gift; enjoy it as much as you can. It's like the wind, or sunshine, or the change of the seasons. It's here, then it's gone.

The Swinging Pendulum (Yowie resumes)

It had to be the times, but I still can't fully account for how we got away with so much right there in plain view of anyone who wanted to look. Especially considering the stricter social mores that preceded that period, and those that the society slithered back to soon after. Still, why didn't neighbors and sensible townspeople rise up one evening and come *viztin'* with flaming torches, pitchforks and cudgels, snarling dogs straining at their tethers, and put a stop to this unbridled depravity in their midst? The occasional wails in the night: Were those moans of sexual titillation, drug-induced delirium, or cries of genuine pain and fear?

How much more dare you provoke these people? Remember, Oregon had been a sanctuary for the Ku Klux Klan throughout the 1920s and well into the '30s. One could argue it was the vigorous response to the rise of international fascism that finally beat back the Klan and stuffed it in a basement closet. Here we were, barely a generation later, part of a conspicuous, noisy minority of mainstream society, a little more out front and in your face than most, figuratively fucking with their basic identities by mocking the President, Old Glory, the Establishment, and the military—and literally fucking their daughters, sisters. Now and then, their wives, too…

Hold on Mister, did you just flip off Jesus <u>and</u> Merka? Well, get the roofin' tar t'heatin', boys! We got us a live one, here! Hyuh, hyuh, hyuh…

Considering the interval between the late 1960s, and 1973 or '74—no more than eight years—that period was very permissive, indeed. Surely the Vietnam (undeclared) War was the initial focus on which to rally our generation's oppositional stance, our often-as-not If-you-got-it-flaunt-it defiance. As we became emboldened in our evolving tactics to resist the draft, gum up the machine and bring the war to a halt, we learned to cultivate and take pride in other counter-mainstream-Merkan identities, as well. In short order, we grew the cojones to oppose the war and promote Native American issues. Or Black empowerment. Or women's empowerment. Or solidarity with gays and lesbians. Or Zoroastrian Cannibals for Cannabis, you name it. Hell, everybody had rights. There was no end to the possibilities.

The gates had been flung open, Pandora forever loosed from her chamber. Some of it was as crackpot as it gets, but on the whole, commandeering the right to flaunt ourselves as we saw fit, to reinvent ourselves in ways antithetical to a seriously flawed "business as usual" social model was an incredibly liberating experience, an essential aspect of the hippie ethos. If you had recently come to question the legitimacy of the government to provide meaningful models for life, well hey, the sky was the limit as to alternative lifestyles to try out.

The prominent mantra of the day was Take control of your life. Why let the Leviathan define you? What better way than to set aside old roles and try out new identities? Who do you want to be? extends to Who do you want to be <u>with</u>? Who, simultaneously, do you want to be in any relationship with? I seriously doubt anyone who lived through that time as a young adult, and had the courage to venture out into that alternative realm, can say they are sorry they experienced that time. It was a major paradigm shift in society. For a while, anyway.

It was surely the times, a fairly brief period in which a combination of circumstances permitted the relaxing of many of the social constraints. Large chunks of mainstream America came to question who we were as citizens, as human beings, and to find solidarity in resistance to that utterly irredeemable war in Vietnam, but much else of what we thought mainstream America stood for. To be sure, many in the drop-out community were apolitical, an unconscionable copout, I always felt. Virtually everyone in the Sub was actively involved in the anti-war effort, apoliti-Pollo being an exception. I'd earned my stripes in Tucson, late-1967/early-'68, picketing the federal courthouse weekly, and being the 3rd person in Tucson to publicly cut my connection to the Selective Service System.

In early December, 1967, I attended the demonstration in front of the Selective Service office at which first David Rehfield, then Bradley Littlefield became the first citizens of Tucson to publicly renounce association with the war machine. Later that same day, the "rabble" (as John Adams, second President of the US, liked to call us) were able to impede, temporarily at least, a Gray Dog full of clueless-patriot conscripts from being driven off to the nearest military base for induction and subsequent cannon fodder.

In the *Tucson Daily Citizen* photo (see following page), I'm standing because the sneering bus driver was revving the engine, trying to intimidate us (and managing, I might add). You never know when one of these guys goes berserk-o, "accidently" releasing the brake and squashing seventeen hippies, like so many possums on the freeway. Everyone else in the shot is sitting. Judy Abbey, third or fourth wife of famed Southwest author Edward Abbey, is shown on the right, fourth back in profile kneeling, Malcolm Simpson is in front facing away, his sign not visible. Bradley Littlefield with his back to the bus facing the camera, glasses. My sign says, WAR IS THE ENEMY, NOT PEOPLE, an appropriate sentiment, I thought.

Three days later I answered the door to two FBI agents who wanted to check me out—and to deliver a subpoena to appear in court. I was so paranoid they were there to sniff any pot connection, I was almost glad it was about my participation in the demonstration—after all, that was never intended to be a covert act. At the appointed occasion, I was charged with unlawful assembly, disturbing the peace, and creating a public nuisance(?)—I'm not sure about the third misdemeanor. I was the first to be tried among seventeen indictments. I had legal counsel donated to the cause and the trial was very straightforward. I was found guilty of two of the three misdemeanors. Since I was about to graduate from the university and my record was clean, I got two years' probation. The

TUESDAY, DECEMBER 5, 1967

Thou Shalt Not Move

Anti-draft demonstrators temporarily defied the takeoff of a busload of inductees from a downtown Scott Avenue departure point yesterday afternoon but the bus and a swarm of city policemen won out. Violence during the demonstration stopped short of bloodshed. (Citizen Photo by Bill Hopkins) judge would not permit the Vietnam War or its ramifications to be introduced into the court's proceedings.

My draft classification was I-Y, a low conscription probability (in the event of direct homeland attack) owing to a moderate blood deficiency I'd inherited from my mother. Nevertheless, I felt acutely uncomfortable in my "privileged" status, especially having watched my 20-year-old comrade, Bradley, torch his card. The solution, of course, was to sever my connection as well. On February 23, 1968, I made a brief public presentation reading the following letter at a large antiwar rally on campus:

February 23, '68

Local Board Number Seven
Selective Service System
106 E. Roosevelt St.
Phoenix, Arizona

Dear Friends:

Enclosed is my draft card. Please don't take the trouble to send it back to me. After long months of grappling with the dilemma, I've decided—conclusively decided—that the only way I can begin to be honest with myself and my fellow man is to refuse to co-operate with military conscription in any form. You probably don't understand that (at least I make that assumption inasmuch as the nature of your work precludes an understanding of non-cooperation). You probably think that peace is a nice word but one which is very difficult to apply in a complicated and greedy world such as we live in. Well, I concede that it's a fairly greedy and complicated world. But I, myself, don't exercise much influence over the world, you see, I only exercise control over my own behavior, and influence the few people I come in contact with—which is part of the reason for this letter.

Peace, of course, is a word. But more, it's a state of mind; it's a way of life (note: <u>life</u> not death). And that the only way this state of mind, this way of life, is going to come about is for people—just like you and I (sic)—to start living it. And that it represents a monstrous contradiction to say that I or anyone else must take up arms in pursuit of peace or freedom or any other grossly overused abstraction mankind universally regards as beneficial.
I can't be at peace with myself or the people I confront daily if I continue to carry a card that says I tacitly condone a violent and vengeful and inhumane solution to the world's problems.

Oh, I suppose I could make my case for this action: over 50% of each tax dollar goes toward war armament (ludicrously called "Defense") while thousands, perhaps millions of the world's people go hungry, that we, as a nation represent about 8% of the world's population yet we annually consume some 60% of the world's saleable raw materials, and so on, and so on. But you know all these things already, don't you? So where's the justice? We are all brothers, aren't we? Not just the ones that (sic) live in Flagstaff or Georgia but the one that live in Greece. And China, as well.

Rationally, I just couldn't point a gun at someone because someone else said he constituted a threat to my race or my ideology or the arbitrarily defined geography of the land in which I was born. I didn't choose to be born (here or anywhere else) and I probably won't choose the time or manner of my death. Those aren't the factors to be concerned about. Neither pride nor sorrow:

they just happen. It's that period of unspecified time in between that concerns me. And you, whether you know it or not.

And please don't delude yourself into thinking there is someone over in Vietnam defending my right to make these comments. Because I'd make these comments... wherever I was born and under whatever regime. That person in Vietnam is killing. He is subverting others (<u>his</u> brothers, too!) by brutalizing them.

Oh, there are so many words to say but they are only words after all... and words only take on meaning through action, after all.

Yours in Peace,
Carl A.(Tony) Cole
739 N. 7th Ave.
Tucson,
Arizona
U.S.A.
<u>World</u>

Some of those population-vs-consumption numbers are probably off, there's a syntactic faux pas here and there, and there's a cringe-inducing earnestness about it, but the content stands fairly consistent with my current thoughts—45 years later. For a 26-year-old initiate to the world of raw public defiance of the American government, this was heady stuff, a great release. Talk about *Take control of your own life,* this was big time.

The consequence turned out to be lighter than it could have been. As anticipated, my medical classification was changed from I-Y to I-A, Delinquent, a typical SS strategy. Then, to test the resistor's mettle, they usually tried to draft you, at which time the malefactor had to choose underground/Canada or refusal to be inducted/jail time for non-compliance with SS. Or eat your words and get promptly shipped off to the slaughter. The infrequent times this latter option happened would be accompanied by fanfare and war-monger gloating.

I thought this through and decided I would make them put me in jail. My conscience was going to require my country to incarcerate me. However, Fate is a curious critter. For reasons beyond my ken, the summons never came, and the SS opted not to continue the process by trying to induct me. Bradley Littlefield served at least half-year in the Safford, AZ, minimum security Federal Prison for his crimes against the State. Go figure.

The Lilliputians, Malcolm and Mudra, got a stipend to stay involved in organizing the resistance. Artie Bonnet was a serious resister and may also have been subsidized; outside of academics, mobilizing resistance to the war seemed to be all-compelling to him. Still, the Yellow Submarine's mission statement, our collective modus operandi, if we were to have one, would more accurately approximate Any excuse for a party! than Bring down the established order! We were never disciplined enough to be sustained revolutionaries.

Of course if every Merkan fully acted out his/her defiance in his/her own manner, the social unit would begin to resemble an bomb exploding in slow motion; the logical extension would have been the disintegration of the microcosm of the Sub, as well as the macrocosm of the Untied Snakes of Amrika, or for that matter the whole international framework. There needs to be somesort of social organization for the revolutionaries/ eccentrics/ oppositionals to react against. The complete disintegration of America, flawed though she certainly was and is, was not the goal. Just the belligerent, acquisitive, rapine, greedy aspects. Thus, it turned out to be pragmatic to have a familiar, mainstream identity or two to fall back on when flaunting one's eccentricities at the corrupt, immoral, and nepotistic Dominant Narrative.

Though a Oneforall-Allforone commune seemed a viable option

at the time, that oppositional stance to the DN wouldn't ultimately turn out to be a successful career move for most of the revelers. Sure as hell, all the institutions we railed against had endured assaults of one form or another their entire history, from decades (e.g., bastions of Corporatism: Exxon, and Coca Cola), to centuries (the sanctity of nation-statehood), to millennia (the Catholic Church). Those well-entrenched seats of power weren't about to succumb to our carnival onslaught. And, as we know, verily they didn't.

Turn around, go back down, back to where you came
Babylon is laid to waste, Egypt buried in her shame
The mighty men are all beaten down,
their kings are fallen by the way
Oh God, pride of man, broken in the dust again...

Turn around, go back down, back to where you came
Terror is on every side; lo our leaders are dismayed
For those who place their faith in fire,
their faith in fire shall be repaid
Oh God, pride of man, broken in the dust again.

Pride of Man, Quicksilver Messenger Service

Notes of Rage (from the zeitgeist of the day)

Amrika, you are a juggernaut careening down the tracks, out of control. You must be stopped; this I know as sure as I live. You are quite mad. As I try to analyze what power you wield that is so lethal, I realize that it is economic control over the vital support systems that enslave us all. By being tied to money. By equating money with the value of life. By putting a price on life. By having to buy food to eat, shelter, a place to call home, transportation, the ability to communicate with the rest of the world. And by having to submit to a period of indentured servitude in order to provide these basic requirements for one's family. Worst of all, by being compelled to strive against other human beings to safeguard these essentials—all of us unwittingly pitted against each other. Ignorant armies clashing by night… Wealth, real value, is not money!

To release your death-grip from the throttle, I take the path of ignoring your existence: Satyagraha. I become enslaved only to the extent that I am dependent on the manufactured essentials for survival. Therefore I minimize my expenditures. It is perhaps not possible, in today's world, to become completely independent of money—there are simply skills and services that are not free and cannot be duplicated on call—but it is staggering to realize how little is truly needed, if doing without currency of the realm is the object. Then, of course, the less money you need, the less energy you have to devote to acquiring it—in my experience, usually a drag.

To whatever extent possible, removing oneself from the means of production and consumption, not to mention the clutches of the Internal Revenue Service, and Selective Service System—in short, the attempt to manage your behavior—you deny the primacy, if not the very existence, of an authority over your life in so repugnant a form as nation-statehood.

Amrika, the one thing I hold in common with the rabid, wild-eyed, Weatherman kamikaze guerrilla and the listless, furtive, chameleon stoner is the awareness of the inequality and the oppression, and the conviction and intention to bring you to your knees. This is no longer politics in the sense of this or that candidate, certainly not reflexively this or that party. That hasn't worked sufficiently in my lifetime for me to have any faith in it. The fact that our means of governance could be more repressive and fascist than it is is a very low bar of acceptability, and no reason to acquiesce from pressing for ever more equitable social conditions.

Amrika, it's not too late to recreate our core identity as more compassionate, tolerant, and egalitarian; less greedy, acquisitive, and profligate. We must redefine growth. The old economy "grew" through plundering the earth's resources, along with its prodigal despoilment and waste. In the Post-Petroleum economy growth, ever doing more with less, will have to consider its carbon footprint, and the other heretofore externalized costs. We're not going to be able to indulge waste in the new economy. It's not going to be as much fun as the old rip-city, cut-and-run growth. This new growth will be dependent on other characteristics than extraction of Earth's finite resources. Like it or not, we are witnessing a shrinkage of our options, an energy descent, *n'est-ce pas'*?

Amrika, it is too late, isn't it?

> *Get your motors running, set out on that highway*
> *Looking for adventure and whatever comes our way*
> *Yeah, I gotta go and make it happen*
> *Catch the world in a love embrace*
> *Fire all of my guns at once, and explode into space*
> *Like a true nature's child, we were born, born to be wild*
> *We'll fly so high, we're never gonna die…*

> *Born to Be Wild*, **Steppenwolf**

The Saga of the Mamarone

I'm having to dredge pretty deeply, but here's what I can cough up. I think it was late-spring of '69 when some folks passing through hit us up with an offer we couldn't refuse: They were shy of cash and needed to sell their 1946 International Harvester 1 1/2- ton truck (in good shape; they'd driven it here from central California, hadn't they? Ok, it could use a tune up...), and they were open to negotiations. Meanwhile, it was true we'd considered obtaining a general-purpose truck. To sweeten the deal, they were willing to throw in something like 80 hits of pure blotter acid. As I recall, the $145 full-purchase payment turned out to be in reality a down payment, the truck costing several times the initial price in repairs: rings, valves, brakes, rebuilt radiator, tires, virtually every gasket needed replacing—some serious money within the first two or three months of ownership. There was still an IH sales and service office in Eugene, mostly for tractors, but they were delighted to have an old-timer to work on. No doubt, we punched their meal ticket for a while.

At some point during this process this old beater of a truck acquired the name Mamarone. I'm pretty sure it was a corruption of some obscure Dr. John lyric, Mama Roux, she was the queen of the bayou... that Quarrel had seized on, though how or why are lost in the ensuing haze. She came to us with a plywood box built on the stake frame on the steel flatbed, riding on a single rear axle of four wheels. There was a hatch for easy access, and a couple thicknesses of carpet on the floor so people could lounge in back while traveling from place to place in relative comfort, as well as privacy.

On one such occasion most of the Submariners decided to attend a rock concert in Corvallis. On the appointed day we got our heads ready—as in preparation for any task—gathered our accoutrements, and loaded into the truck—three in front maximum, Tumor driving most of the time, the rest like a bunch of migrant workers all crammed in back. Except this was more like a Cheech-and-Chong movie where billows of smoke waft out through the cracks at every stop. Taking 99W out of Junk City, this whole trip would have taken less than an hour at normal highway speeds. Not the Mamarone: 45 mph, 50 max. We needed to break in our rebuilt engine slowly, gently; traffic could just pile up behind us. Miles per gallon of fuel? Don't even ask. Fuel efficiency was way down the list of concerns; recall, it's only from the benefit of hindsight that we can determine America's peak domestic petroleum production occurred around 1972. As of 1968, there was still "no end in sight."

We'd pull over at the waysides to stretch our legs, urinate in the bushes, trade places with the throne sitters up front. The scenario we never wanted to talk about was, if that ol' gal had ever flipped over with 6 or 8 of us hunkered in the back, nothing to hold onto except each other's sorry asses, nothing to protect us but a flimsy ½ inch plywood box nailed to a 2x4 staked frame, it would have been mashed and mangled hippies for seventy-five feet, not a pretty image...

Where was that concert held, Gill Auditorium/Stadium? You paid $10, or $12 to come and go as you liked through at least three major acts, with a couple of regional bands thrown in. Steve Miller Band, Youngbloods, and, I dunno, maybe Paul Butterfield Blues Band. By about half way through this rock extravaganza, having smoked up since before we left home several hours before, it all got a little fuzzy, this despite having been in daily training for just such an occasion. The Mamarone must've hauled our weary tails home very early the next morning. I couldn't tell you; I was beyond the pale by then.

She hauled material and personnel to and from the Country Fair at least one year, that first one, called the Renaissance Faire, staged on some beautiful acreage just off of South Willamette St. She was also used to transport the ingredients for granola to the Sub's marginally copasetic "kitchen", and the finished product in 50~60 lb. plastic garbage-can loads to be distributed to the health-food co-ops around Eugene.

On another occasion, 10 or 12 of us attended the first-run showing of "The Yellow Submarine" movie on Willamette St. downtown. Since we were celebrating our namesake, we decided to drop as a group and go to the movies! It was one of those films of animated Beatles performing some excellent music, sight gags and plays on words to Peter Max's exquisite animation, which was spectacularly psychedelic on mescaline.

I'm often uncomfortable being that wrecked in public. While I generally manage all right, I imagine everyone can tell I'm whacked out of my mind. On this occasion, however, despite the Blue Meanies, it was a delightful experience. At the end of the 90-minute film, when the lights came up, it became apparent (via the eyes, the "portals to the soul") that some 2/3 of the audience were likewise experiencing seriously altered consciousness—above and beyond the magic of Peter Max and the Fab Four.

The Mamarone was the only means of conveyance capable of ferrying that many of us altogether, anywhere. She was a great old truck; I don't know what happened to her but I'm pretty sure it was death by a thousand repair bills.

Rock and Roll

It seemed important to acknowledge the cultural icons of the age, to count coup on all the respected rock groups that passed through the area—and let's face it, most of them stopped off at Eugene or Corvallis. All the good ones had some unique feature, some redeeming quality, like a signature sound worth offering up one's hard-come-by money, and exposing oneself for a couple hours to 125 decibels (WHAT did you say?). One of my favorites of the day was Country Joe and the Fish, a Bay Area jug band that had discovered the wonders of LSD. I remember Xmas of 1967, pre-Sub by 7~8 months, was made more interesting by "Electric Music for Mind and Body," whose lyrics from this and their second album stated explicitly that President LBJ and certain cabinet members should take acid, strongly implying the country would be better off, if they did. We saw them on two passes through Eugene and were mightily entertained both times.

Parenthetically, it's interesting to track rock groups pre and post-LSD. The Beach Boys by Good Vibrations were definitely post. The Stones maybe as far back as Aftermath—"Paint it Black" has got whacked-out Brian Jones all over it—surely by Flowers, or Between the Buttons. The Beatles by Rubber Soul or maybe Revolver. It is a matter of historical record that "Sgt. Pepper's Lonely Hearts' Club Band" pretty much pole-axed the rock world. Nobody'd seen anything like that, ever. Thanks to George Martin, their musical advisor/big-picture director, they could allow their psychically skewed musical ideas to flourish.

Then, there's ol' Kenny Rogers, whose bread 'n' butter persona has been pure cracker millionaire country boy for most of his career. However, he started his musical career a suitably twisted stone-freak lead singer of The First Edition when he crooned these acid-inspired lyrics:

...I tripped on a cloud and fell eight miles high
I tore my mind on a jagged sky
I just dropped in to see what condition my condition was in...

I remember the song from the time. It was a moderate hit for them, and I wish to assure the reader, nobody hearing the song in the day would have doubted the condition Kenny's condition was in.

I saw the Doors, in Morrison's post-Miami-arrest/pre-trial period for lewd conduct/indecent exposure. The band was professional, adequate, but Morrison gave a petulant, desultory performance. I think the Lizard King was by this time beyond the pale of polite social engagement, and into the pail of self-absorption, ultimately leading to self-loathing—on that ol' downward spiral. He'd toe-tested the waters of Nepenthe before. He was no stranger to pushing the margins of self-indulgence. What is that, too much adulation, too quick? Intimidated by the limelight, fearful you won't be able to live up to the expectations of your adoring fans?

Steve Miller made an annual pass through Eugene, it seemed. He wasn't a flashy performer, just a rock-solid musician with a long string of hits. The Beach Boys visited Eugene on one of the summer festivals, sans Brian, of course, but including Carl, Mike Love, and a yet-sentient Dennis: What can I say? Vapid lyrics, interesting melodies, and amazing harmonies. Here's one that is pure First Wave redux, Chuck Berry's instantly recognizable, signature guitar riff intro, and car-adventure lyrics—but penned by Brian:

Well, she got her daddy's car
and she cruised to the hamburger stand now
Seems she forgot all about the library like she told her old man now
With the radio blasting she goes cruising just as fast as she can now
And she'll have fun, fun, fun till her daddy takes the T-bird away

Fun, fun, fun, The Beach Boys

The biggest coup I counted from those daze—late-fall 1968—was seeing the Grateful Dead, the first of many occasions, on campus in the Senior Ballroom upstairs in the Urp Memorial Student Union, a venue that couldn't have accommodated more than about 500 people. The room was quite packed and the band was too loud, and truth to tell, my radar hadn't yet been attuned to their style of sustained, stony, free-floating improvisation. By the second or third time, I saw them in Mac Court where people could spread out, and the music was starting to make sense.

Ken Kesey, our local luridly loquacious literary luminosity, lived just a few miles southeast of town. He was an early intimate of theirs, who introduced them to Owsley Stanley, and helped stage the early San Francisco electric Kool-Aid acid concert/be-ins with the Dead before acid was criminalized. Between 1965 and '67 Owsley cooked up more than a million and a quarter hits of acid (Wikipedia) providing a significant catalyst to the emergence of flower children, and the anti-war, anti-authoritarian counterculture. The Dead would come to Eugene, a quick hop up from Marin County, pretty much on any pretext Kesey could conjure up.

At the time, I mostly sought out straight ahead, unambiguous rock'n'roll a la the Stones, the Who (who?), Quicksilver, Big Brother, Credence, Jefferson Airplane, Cream/Blind Faith/Traffic, Steppenwolf, Steve Miller, the Kinks, Zep, and of course, Jimi. The softer end of rock would include the Beatles; Buffalo Springfield; the Dead; Crosby, Stills, and Nash; Youngbloods; Neil Young; and the Byrds.

The Doors occupy a unique, depending-on-the-song-exotic niche. Songs like *5 to 1*, *The End* and their incredible interpretation of the Willie Dixon warhorse, *Back Door Man* have the power to put the listener in touch, as if hypnotically, with his/her subconscious, primordial self, without half trying. In "The Music's Over," Morrison piqued our budding environmental awareness with these words:

> *What have they done to the earth?*
> *What have they done to our fair sister?*
> *Ravaged and plundered and raped her and bit her,*
> *Stuck her with knives in the sight of the dawn*
> *Pinned her with fences and dragged her down*
> *I hear a very gentle sound*
> *With our ears down to the ground*

(loud, alarmed) *We want the world and we want it...*
(softly, almost whispered)   *now...*
(tentatively, questioning)   *now?...*

then comes a thunderous, apocalyptic NA-OOWW! at the peak of his vocal range, before slowly trailing off, surely one of the two or three most exquisite, full-throated shrieks in rock. Talk about use of the human voice to express a primordial emotion. A mere word becomes a platform for pandemonium. That boy flat be channeling the Fiends of Hell, I shit you not!

Then, there were the one (sometimes two)-album wonders: Vanilla Fudge, Moby Grape, Jeff Beck/Rod Stewart (Truth), Iron Butterfly's In A-Gadda-Da Vida, Procol Harum's astonishing second album, Shine on Brightly; Joe Cocker's first album, With a Little Help from my Friends, Aqualung by Jethro Tull, and a suitably twisted social satire called Sanders' Truck Stop. And let us not forget a trio calling themselves Blue Cheer. Recognizing the band's name was code for a popular brand of LSD of the day—again, with an Owsley connection—gave a key perspective to appreciating the band's tortured, feels-like-10-minute version of Eddie Cochran's classic, Summertime Blues. Still no word from Procter and Gamble as to the expropriation of the name of their popular laundry detergent for a tasteless, odorless, mind-shattering, psychedelic chemical ingested by a bunch of degenerates...

It is no exaggeration to say that much of our lives played out with the music represented by these and other artists as a background. Hell, a good deal of the time it was the foreground as well; it was all around us. This period corresponded with the arrival of the Second Wave of rock'n'roll. It was a huge wave; we were awash in some of the most innovative, creative singing/songwriting/musicianship in rock history, certainly of our age.

We wallowed in it, conducting lengthy "research" on incipient misogyny in early Stones lyrics, for example (preliminary report: It's there in spades), or nuanced interpretations of abstruse Morrison passages, or coded references to genitalia and the sex act in blues/rock; you get the idea. It was an endlessly rich source of metaphoric references (Ain't fattening no more frogs for snakes), epigrams (Meet the new boss; same as the old boss), and pithy comments (You don't need a weatherman to know which way the wind blows) to lend depth and poignancy to real-life contexts. Music became an integral part of the context for many, a framework, a skeleton on which to hang life's events in those

        goo
              dol
                    daze.

* * * * *

And when my mind is free
you know a melody can move me
and when I'm feelin' blue
the guitar's comin' through to soothe me...

Gimme the beat, boys, to soothe my soul
I wanna get lost in your rock and roll
and drift away

    Drift Away, Dobie Gray

Yowie & Gina,
Thanksgiving 1969

When the music's over…

At some point, the music must come to an end. All beginnings contain the seeds of their own endings. It is only when concepts avoid or transcend such notions as origins, that finalities can be dispensed with—patently not the case for most of the ebbs and flows of our lives. I did what I could; I stuck with it for two years, four months. I lasted longer than anyone else, even though torn and frayed remnants of the old Yellow Sub, rudderless, listed on for another four months or so. It had devolved into cheap rent, a proverbial crashpad, for too many people with too little in common.

Gina had seen it long before me. It took me a while to figure out that she was hanging around because of me. There just wasn't much left of group effort/common meals, anything like that anymore. It was this faction against those factions with a few non-aligns thrown in, a fucking microcosm of the world at large. Ack! Finally, she left. She rented a room in a house across town, and must still have been working at the New World to pay the bills, I suppose. Chanren had just departed the month before, his second time, with Lindy Button.

It didn't feel good anymore. I couldn't make it work. I stretched it out until early December 1970, mostly trying to figure out what I was going to do out there where basics suddenly cost real money. I had coasted on very little money all this time because all the Sub costs were defrayed by all the members. And the granola economy paid all the Sub bills as well as disbursed a little income to those who had put in hours above the minimum required.

Now it was time to put the Sub behind me, get a real job, and like the rest of the world, start paying some real bills. So I followed Gina out; she was willing to forgive me my sins—at the time anyway—and thought we might make a life of it. We were fortunate enough to serendipitously stumble into the opportunity of managing/care-taking a funky, rundown hippie motel/hostel on the coastal headlands between Florence and Yachats. What young adult wouldn't seize the chance to stay, rent/utilities free, right on the ocean? It was my first, sustained land's-end experience. This exquisite environment turned out to be the ideal place for us to settle in for a while and take our bearings. To reflect, and make a baby.

* * * * *

'All hands on deck, we've run afloat,' I heard the captain cry
'Explore the ship, replace the cook; let no one leave alive!'
Across the straits, around the horn, how far can sailors fly?
A twisted path, our tortured course and no one left alive
We sailed for parts unknown to man where ships come home to die
No lofty peak, no fortress bold could match our captain's eye
Upon the seventh seasick day we made our port of call
A sand so white, and sea so blue, no mortal place at all

We fired the gun, and burnt the mast, and rowed from ship to shore
The captain cried, we sailors wept; our tears were tears of joy
Now many moons and many Junes have passed since we made land
A salty dog, this seaman's log; your witness, my own hand.

A Salty Dog, Procol Harum

Conclusions

1) Only two couples, among quite a few, ever entered the Sub, stayed awhile, and left paired to each other, as they had come. One was the curious couple of Frimpton de Monumency and his blond-haired child concubine, Joy (and doncha just know she was!). Up from California, looking for a place to settle, they had the Mann Act written all over them.

Also known as the White Slave Trade Act, if the Supreme Court hadn't struck it down the previous year, lecherous ol' Frimpton coulda spent the rest of his life in prison. This was a grotesquely racist 1910 Act of Congress forbidding the transport of women/ girls across state lines for sexual purposes—though the framers of the act preferred the term, debauchery, "… for purposes of debauchery," which, to me, has a decidedly more sinister, lurid, perhaps degraded connotation than mere sex. As if getting hosed on the other side of the state line was a whole lot more injurious to the "victim" than here, on this side. Huh?

The two most prominent convictions since its enactment involved a high-profile uppity black man and a white woman. The first to do time for a Mann Act violation was the superb black prizefighter Jack Johnson, a full century ago. That which white, American manhood could not do to this man stand up, face to face, in the ring, it could damn well do in court. America simply wasn't ready in those days to countenance the notion of some black buck slipping his mammoth-trunk schlong into a demure, lily-white honey pot, despite the fact that in Johnson's case the woman was reputed to be a hooker who was only too happy to accompany him from New Jersey to New York for more of that Black Mamba. It's not recorded whether he paid her in dollars or inches, but the point was she was hardly an ingénue. Anti-Miscegenation Laws in 30 states, even prohibiting consenting-adults from free-will sexual commingling of the "races," were upheld until 1948 (Wikipedia).

The other prominent Mann Act conviction was in 1962, when the country was still racist enough to lock away Chuck Berry for 20 months, a serious crimp in his career, because he escorted an under-age groupie across a state line with the clear intent of fucking the brains out of the willing and eager girl—probably building her resume. In this act he was behaving as thousands of other rock performers, uh, musicians, um, entertainers of any stripe, had done and would continue to do beyond counting, on the road. Those are the spoils of being "charismatic," even to a limited audience.

I don't think Frimpton and Joy stuck around more than about three months. They were a little vague as to ages; she was introduced as 18; we later found out she was barely 15. Frimpton was a street-savvy hustler who was protective of his honey but otherwise reasonably jovial, cooperative. He might've been late-50s, or even early-60s. Where did he hail from, St Louis? New Orleans? She was pure SoCal, in a hurry to be an adult, and not quite able to pull it off, except between the sheets, I suppose. We helped them get acclimated to Eugene, at which time they found jobs and moved into their own apartment. She was conspicuously preggers by then.

The other, earlier exception to the couples' outcome was Malcolm and Mudra, who might have stayed ten months. By that time Malcolm's paranoia that Mudra was engaging in the ol' in and out on the sly with one or another of her admirers had pretty much tainted our interactions. I'll be the first to admit I lusted after sweet, coy, little Mudra, and had an opportunity presented itself, I would not have hesitated to step up to the plate, bat at the ready. But I wasn't so lust stricken that I plotted maneuvers or contrived schemes to peel her off from Malcolm's scrutiny. Cuckolded husbands sometimes act irrationally. He was short and tightly wound, a bad combination, in my estimation. Besides, there was an ongoing panoply of far less socially complicated womanhood willing to be cultivated, without having to fixate on sweet little Mudra.

These two couples, the only ones who made it out intact, were the exceptions that proved the rule. For virtually everyone who stayed a while, the attraction to have carnal knowledge with not just one, but several other partners (presumably sequentially, but who am I to judge?) became more than the pair-bound couple could endure. Once that sexual intimacy was newly entered into, a psychic barrier was surpassed and you were somehow, some quantum degree closer to that other person.

Initial members Chanren and Anita, married four years and with a child, lasted less than eight months in the Yellow Submarine. Double T and Gina, married for two years, were no longer an exclusive couple within days of their arrival. For Ned and Dana, it was probably hours; I was (on) her welcoming committee, if memory serves. Quarrel, wife and child endured perhaps days before any pretense of monogamy was tossed, surprising no one since they'd had an open marriage from the beginning—something like six years.

Anita's Tale, Pt. 2

When I was a little girl I always dreamed of someday growing up, finding a husband, getting married, having a family and living happily ever after!!! Yup!!! That was my dream!!!!

When it was decided that we should go to Oregon, I must have had many mixed feelings. I certainly didn't want to leave all my relatives in Phoenix—but we were a family with a tiny newborn baby. It would be an adventure.

How naïve could I have been!!! In my mind, I thought we could be a happy married family while living with all the various people in the commune. In April 1969 I took Karisma back to Phoenix to celebrate her first birthday with Grandma and Grandpa and all my family. When we came back to the commune, I sadly learned that Chanren was not on the "same page" about marriage. He informed me that he had been seeing a girl while I was gone. He worked nights at the coffee house, and often came home way past the closing hours. I should have seen it all coming.

My solution to that horrible (to me) situation was to forgive him and for the three of us to move out and get a place of our own. We looked at several rentals but I soon came to realize that it simply wasn't going to work. Our marriage was over. It seemed like my whole world had come to an end. My dreams from my childhood were dashed!! About the end of May 1969 I decided to take Karisma and move out on our own.

Chanren stayed on at the commune. I stayed with friends until I found a place to rent and got a job working at a daycare center. I wanted to stay in Eugene so we could both share time with Karisma. I remember dropping in the commune occasionally, walking through Hendricks Park with Karisma in the stroller. My folks came up to Eugene and wanted us to move back to Phoenix. I think they were disappointed that I said no.

Marriage and communal living just were not compatible. As I recall, there were five marriages at the commune that all ended up in divorce!!

The times, and certainly our household, were not favorable to relationships that were presumed to be preemptively locked away. Such notions carried zero weight among the hormonally charged swinging hammers of the Yellow Submarine. Which was A-ok with Stan and, especially, Phillipa Thompson, who expressed eagerness for some serial sexuality, having just opened their house to the wiles of the communal experience. After watching it go on around them a while, she intended to make up for lost time. The normal response of the too-long repressed, one supposes. The Thompsons backed out of the communal experiment after only about three months; I don't suppose their marriage was much bolstered as a result.

2) If only two couples made it through the Sub intact, and so many couples came to the Sub that didn't survive, it follows that the communal environment must have been better suited to "single," i.e., not just unmarried but unattached, adults over the long run. This finding seems to be corroborated by the number of single people who left the commune in order to form a pair bond, become a couple. Chanren came with Anita and Karisma, their daughter, and left with Terra. Later, he returned as a single only to leave again, this time with Lindy. Pollo started as a single and left with Dana. Tumor came as a single and left with Katy. Geary came as a single and left with Gale. Quarrel came with Doris and Luke, their son, rooted through most of the women before leaving with Deedee—to save the marriage—later to return as a single again. I came as a single and engaged many brief, and a few not so brief, liaisons before finally leaving in pursuit of Gina. I had resisted it long enough. It was definitely time: Retirement from this worthy social experiment, Yellow Submarine duty, after two years four months.

3) Here's as good a place as any to weigh notions of Success, and Failure. Did the Yellow Submarine contribute to, or detract from "the Greater Good," assuming we could come up with what this Greater Good might entail? Was it worthwhile? Just as soon as I am provided the measuring device—a tape measure, a stop watch?—I will commence rendering verdicts forthwith. I remind the reader that there were no stated, codified goals from the outset. Given the malleability and porosity of the Yellow Submarine-as-organization, it's remarkable the group maintained as much cohesion, for as long as it did.

We may not have had any formalized goals, but I think most of us operated with some implicit goals, for example, an understanding to pool our individual strengths and share in the tasks necessary to feed ourselves and pay for rent/utilities. We had an implied socio-economic pact, a willingness, in the early months anyway, to explore new strategies. We would use our collective skills and energies to minimize the need for outside jobs. Those first ten or twelve people had known each other or knew about each other, in some cases, for years. Friendships, and the trust that accompanied them, went back a long time. Many of those bonds had accrued substance and reliability over the months and years; it wasn't necessary to define them contractually. The need to do so could itself engender mistrust.

In a previous paragraph and elsewhere I have written of the inherent "openness" of the commune to visitors/guests/new occupants, and the close proximity of the campus and city, as if they were flaws and distractions, and in other negative terms—for valid reasons, perhaps. However, a case can also be made that openness and urban proximity were to some degree beneficial, as well. Without the city as an escape valve for many Sub members, if we had somehow restricted comings and goings of visitors, and even members, the Yellow Submarine could very well have imploded within the first six months. There would have been no Tumor, no Marta, no Gale, Lindy, Elvis, or the rest of the Buttons, and many others. It's that ol' A little is good, too much is bad, and there is no fixed middle ground. A stone freak might say, How you gonna know the happy medium, that dreaded Golden Mean, unless you experience excess?

Without a doubt people left the Sub with scars, psychic or otherwise. I'd say people who lived there for some period of time and didn't acquire any scars were very low-level participants. The thing is, no matter where you are, if you are involved in the events around you, aren't you apt to "earn" a scar or two? Life is a risk, period. Some would argue, the more the risk, the more exciting the life. Show me your scars; I'll show you mine.

I wasn't ever particularly into putting life at risk for the adrenaline rush. Still, I'd subscribe to the idea that a kind of reciprocity occurs in willed participation of events. In short, the ones who were involved in this or that aspect of life in the Sub, and helped give it substance and momentum—as opposed to those who went along for the ride—probably got the most out of it, rewards as well as scars. They were meaningfully affected by the experience in some rough proportion to the level of their involvement in said experience. Wow man, heavy.

Having considered the context of the initial question, Was the Yellow Submarine a success, or failure? I'd say we were unequivocally successful—a success that, like life in general, cloaks but barely sometimes, a variety of failures. For however long each of us coped with the frequently intense interaction, we succeeded: at learning how to share a meal, a bathroom, a house, a lifestyle with sometimes-familiar/intimate partners, while at turns, mere acquaintances. Those lessons were often hard earned, and we are invariably better for the experience. Tempered, like fine high-carbon steel.

I don't suppose I could say we contributed substantially to the so-called Greater Good, however; that may have been too high a bar to clear. But this is not an ethics-based disquisition, in which we'd need to start by defining Greater Good, and so on. Should we do so, I suspect we'd discover many mainstream institutions, then as well as now, putatively serving the public—and falling significantly shy of the mark. Perhaps it's enough to say we of the Yellow Submarine did little to harm this so-called social Good. I frankly believe several of our individual efforts to stop the Vietnam War were socially beneficial and praiseworthy, but they were engaged on a person-by-person basis, and not the efforts of the Sub as a whole.

Regrets? Sure, who doesn't pack around some? Life sometimes presents obstacles, and sometimes we cope with them badly. To my mind, I have no more regrets from that two-year, four-month period than any other comparable time of my life. It was a noble social experiment, made not the less so by being a good deal libidinous and promiscuous in the process.

4) Forty-plus years ago, young adults with little or nothing invested in more orthodox lifestyles were often willing to try out a communal lifestyle. Nothing ventured, nothing gained. It was nothing if not a proverbial learning experience. Those who took communal living seriously quickly learned it was going to be hard work constantly redefining/renegotiating social conditions, terms, beyond mere go along to get along. In an egalitarian, participatory-democracy framework, there is no slacking off when each new context presents a new opportunity to see how you might engage, without assumptions arising from previous roles and contexts. Conversely, to slack off is to disengage. Proxies are rarely allowed; one needs to participate to have a say.

In all probability, projecting forward, it's going to take a compelling event to force the shift in Business-as-usual to make dawn-of-the-21st-century Haves surrender many of our conveniences and "entitlements"—read, "license to consume disproportionately with willful ignorance, and no sense of stewardship of resources for future humans, to say nothing of the well-being of the rest of the biosphere." People are apt to cling ever more desperately to the only social model they've known, no matter how dysfunctional it becomes. Most people appear powerless, mesmerized, zombie-like, continuing to refuse/deny "energy descent" right up to the time our collective folly of profligate consumption triggers precipitous shortages in the petroleum supply, and social collapse is visited upon us.

Until then, we succumb to the lure of personal fulfillment as defined by materialism, and consumption of services, e.g., entertainment, transportation, accommodation, and food services. The material benefits of capitalism are too ubiquitous and hard-wire-identified with core culture to be denied. Given the strength of the Dominant Narrative's message to stay the course, "Don't worry, be happy," no one should be surprised that most of us are in denial. It has been easy to ignore bad news about potential outcomes when it doesn't fit the only operating model we've ever known. Incremental expansion of consumption, comfort, convenience through technological "advances" over our parents' generation, as they had over their predecessors, has occurred in a steady regression over the last 200 years. Nobody wants to give up his/her toys before everybody else does, which is to say, when the Game is over.

Frankly, I'd be sanguine with postponing recognition of the looming Collapse, too, if it weren't for the gathering data that indicate putting off the reckoning will only amplify the slope, and hasten the descent. What I'm suggesting here is, in a world of negative projections for the status quo, something like that communal experience of so long ago may again appeal to people who may in future time no longer be able to live the way we'd all grown up to expect.

It's going to take a continuous reexamination and reconstruction of how we should live, and no longer vis-à-vis other humans exclusively. Now the focus requires humans collectively to approach homeostasis with the rest of the biosphere—despite historic internecine struggle. Since reconciling humanity's true vs. presumed needs, while maintaining the wealth, beauty, and diversity of the biosphere is not likely to be easy, we might as well get moving.

Epilogue

Forty-plus years after the voyage of the Yellow Submarine how do the intrepid survivors account the intervening years?

Geary Button: After leaving the commune, Geary and Gale moved to the southern Oregon coast where Geary had connections for working in the woods. Some 18 months into falling trees, he had a serious accident, and wound up losing a leg. After rehab for a prosthetic leg they moved to Alaska where Geary worked in partnership and independently in truck shops, from repair to design, and build from the ground up. G and G had one child, a daughter, before separating. He now lives in a big house in Eugene—with Jay, Candy— and Jackie, Lark's son! He divides his time between making music, fiddling on many an evening with other strummers and pickers, and working toward completion of his Super-bus, a kind of Further Yet on steroids, to haul himself and bandmates inter-city in impressive style.

Yowell Mebsanuri: Gina and I went on to be the proud parents of three children, all homebirths. With money I earned as an ore truck driver at an open pit copper mine in Globe/Miami, AZ, we bought Oregon Coast Range property, to share with Chanren and Lindy, built a cabin and got an awkward start at rural homesteading, complete with goats, chickens, rabbits, and bees, before Gina and I decided to go our own ways. I taught English in Japan for over 10 years, remarried, and settled in Portland in 1995. Since then, I earned my MA in Applied Linguistics from PSU and wrote two books, *Ragnarok, A Plausible Future* and *Shards a life in pieces*, under the feather name of Tuna Cole (check out ragnarokaplausiblefuture.com). All three of my children have thrived in central Florida, with families of their own. To date I am grandfather to six.

Not bad for a burned-out old hippie.

Elvis Boinker: What have I been doing for the last 40 years? I raised four children: Rachel, Cyrus, Zebidiah, and Miriam. I have five grandchildren, one on the way. After the Sub I worked in the woods with Hoedads, Cougar Mountain Crew, planting, falling trees, trail maintenance, living in Eugene. I worked with Jerry Ferrox, John Sunquist, Ed Whimple, Peter Roscoe, Hal Hartzel, Tom Emmens, Quarrel Stockton, Betsy Whimple and the rest of the Cougar Mountain Crew. Many others that were friends with people at the Sub, and Springfield Creamery. I had an import-export business. Eugene has always been a great place to live, but making a living is something else. Moved to Washington in 1979. Started to work at a carpet upholstery cleaning company. Took over the business, managed it till 1984. I then started working in financial services: term insurance, retirement services, IRAs, financial planning. Then, I started a yacht brokerage in Tacoma, did that for six years. I loved that business; then came the first war, Desert Storm, and the economy went to hell in a hand basket. I could not continue throwing good money after bad, so I closed the business. In 1994 went to work at the Seattle Airport. Started with a friend that was a manager there. And have been working there since. I work as a Skycap on departures, as a subcontractor for American Airlines. I have met people there that I would never have met otherwise. Everyone you could imagine. If they fly, they come thru the hub. There is never a dull moment. You never know who's going to pull up. It keeps it interesting. Brenda lives about two miles from me. We have been divorced since 1988. Still remain friends. Things are good, and it has been a good life so far. Nothing to complain about; it always falls on deaf ears anyway. This is a quick summary: Everyone is healthy and living their lives the best they can! Life is short; enjoy it! No promises of tomorrows. Oh well, that's the way it is.

Chanren Ragman: Where did the Submarine go? As if to accentuate what we had done in the years we lived communally, two separate communal groups at different times arrived in subsequent years out of the American South West seeking the Yellow Submarine. There were two single men from a commune in New Mexico introduced to me by Cleda, probably referred by Jack Ladd. One remained in the area until quite recently. In the second instance James Livingston acted as the go between. Three couples and a young son as well as two single men moved to Eugene and rented two different places while they were here. Their common ritual had been to gather together each New Years Day and hike in the Superstition Mountains (southeast of Phoenix) and drop acid. They stayed in Eugene for years and at least one person has remained.

Considering the sheer numbers of male Yellow Submarine members that went on to work with the Hoedads Tree Planting Collective (or one of its offshoots) in the 1970s, one could conclude that we mostly morphed into that worker owned and operated cooperative. That process began in the summer of 1971 when a majority of the declining crew signed on with John Sunquist (a peripheral member) for a trail maintenance contract in the Cascades near Willamette Pass. The work was vigorous, the pay was good and the mosquitoes were horrendous. I was present in that work crew which lasted about a week. However, Lindy and I were already living up the Mckenzie River where we were house-sitting for a year, which turned into five. During these years I helped start a company importing and distributing Chinese medicinal herbs. I also began Dharma practice, cultivating the Tao. While there we became friends with a loose knit group of folks up and down the river known as the "bus people" due to the fact that they were converting old school buses and large trucks into homes on wheels. From there it was five years of homesteading in the Oregon Coast Range followed by five years of living in a traditional Buddhist Way Place. Three wonderful children arrived through natural childbirths. While living at the monastery I worked at resettling S.E.

Asian refugees ("boat people"). Then five years living in the S.F. Bay area with a short stint (nine months) teaching English in Japan. Followed by a return to the west Oregon coast range homestead and running a Natural foods store for almost 15 years. After retiring I did some international vagabonding.

The Meta-Narrative

The Process of Writing this Book

I've been the default editor/coordinator of this project since we began to take it seriously more than a year ago. This was not accomplished through coup d'etat, or somesort of subterfuge, rather through a lack of anyone else rising to the bait. It made sense for me to take it on, and I'm not complaining.

There had to have been some ground rules from the start, however, or this cooperative effort would soon have been scuttled. Foremost among these precepts was the agreement that no one had the right to edit another's text. This was seen primarily as protection of one's own work—that no one else was going to muck around with your own baby, arbitrarily deciding which passage is extraneous/superfluous, which may stay. It was an important, foundational agreement, fine as far as it went. However, to raise concerns about someone else's writing became pure negotiation with the author holding all the aces. If s/he doesn't agree to your proposed changes, it doesn't get changed. Instantly, the tendency to do your own thing begins to show up in an interesting range of differences. An existential dilemma: How does one edit without, in some cases, the authority to edit?

Another ground rule was that if you contributed some text pertaining to your recollections of the Yellow Submarine, undefined in terms of minimum length—even a couple of paragraphs would suffice—you had a vote, equal to the votes of the other contributors, regardless of the reams produced by any one person. I suppose we were saying, sheer volume of output is a dubious way of evaluating. Since quality of output was such a complicated matter, we went with "Any submission gives you a vote," effectively 1/13 of the voting whole.

As a case in point, it became time to decide a name for our project. Chanren had suggested three titles, I offered two with a common subtitle, but it seemed unfair to present these five as the only candidates when the other contributors might have suggestions of their own. Thus, with a week time limit to solicit additional titles, James Livingston came up with a sixth suggestion. Add another week for the eleven contributors to select their top two choices from the list of six, anticipating there would not be a majority selection without counting a second-choice selection.

Here's that email-ballot process.

Ladies and Gentlemen,

Consider this your time-sensitive official ballot as to the title of our soon-to-be born project. In my opinion, it shouldn't matter the sponsor of this or that proposal, so here are the six title proposals:

1) (The) Yellow Submarine Commune
2) The Yellow Submarine Chronicles
   A multi-voice account of life in a commune
3) RazzaMaTazz
   Shenanigans & High Jinks on Board
   The Yellow Submarine Commune
4) Riding the Wave
   Aboard the Yellow Submarine (Commune)
5) (The) Voyage of the Yellow Submarine
   A multi-voice account of life in a commune
6) Tales of the Yellow Submarine Commune
   Soon to Be a Major Motion Picture

Please vote your first <u>and</u> your second choice. I foresee no more than a plurality winner with just first choice. I'm hoping for a majority vote by the "second choice." If not by second choice, we'll have a run off of the top two vote getters.

Please respond by no later than next Friday, 12/16, 4 pm, but sooner is better.

<u>Morning Glory</u>: please, ask the three Buttons their preferences. Thanks again for your help.
Cheers,
Yowie

In response to this ballot, exactly five contributor/electors chose
(The) Voyage of the Yellow Submarine
a *multi-voice chronicle of life in a commune*

by taking into account the second-choice column to establish the barest of majorities. The take-away from this election of contributors was more than half were unable or chose not to be involved in the naming project. It's probably fair to say most contributors were not so interested in title choices, and perhaps most preferred not to have a hand in the nuts and bolts of the project, as was their prerogative. The point is, it was their choice, not mine. The idea of providing everyone the chance to participate is appropriate on its own, and has the additional benefit of absolving me of any elitist, exclusionary claims.

Another heavily contested aspect of the project has been whether to use real names vs. pseudonyms. I championed the use of assigned names to show one layer of separation, should anyone in months to come take offense at a characterization that could be interpreted as damaging her/his reputation, an affront to dignity, a character impugned, you get the drift. Chanren believed, These are the people who were really involved in these events, so why pussyfoot around the facts, as I see them (my paraphrase)? It was like I'd asked him to compromise an essential "truthfulness" of the story. Presumably, there is the implication that we've got something to hide after all these years, which I don't think any of us feel.

The thing is, no one could predict how this or that family member might react, six months or a year from now, to having their loved one described as vomit-speckled, drooling, and drug addled, or being seen in a photo with someone passing a joint, even if it was 40-plus years ago. Actually, I don't think we describe anyone quite like that, but we certainly could. Anyway, people have been known to lose sleep and feel the need to seek legal counsel at slights one would normally shrug off. It's a curious country and a curious time we are living in. The word, divisive springs to mind. Pseudonyms for all was my motto, and my solution. Most folks either didn't care or bought some variation of my rationale.

A further "understanding" we came to concerned the possibility of contributors responding/taking exception to others' accounts. I pressed for the acknowledgement that this would not take place. It was not difficult for me to imagine our project devolving into a series of tit-for-tats, potentially distracting the story telling into a verbal slug fest of who's account was the "accurate" one. This consideration was largely, though not entirely, adhered to.

The saga of beleaguered brotherhood deserves some ink. Fraternal strife has been the stuff of legend since Biblical times (Cain and Abel), and ancient Greek tragedies. By contrast, the struggle between Chanren and me has continued discontinuously for a mere 68 years—interspersed by many good times, I hasten to add. While the Fates seem to have cast this group account of commune days as the crucible for a battle of wills, the conflict has fallen far short of truly epic standards (thankfully!). Nonetheless, wounds and bloodletting have been inflicted at a higher degree of antagonism than experienced in recent memory. Passions have been aroused.

Can you lay all that at the Altar of Ego? Few would deny that our feeble narrative efforts—along with every other artistic attempt since the Lascaux Cave paintings—are a supreme expression of our egos. I confess without shame, it has been a real rush watching parts of my composition emerge, take on shape and color and a kind of motion—almost life. On occasion, it has been a source of sheer delight.

Yet the book has become the contested territory between two brothers who each have invested creative effort—skin in the game—at cross-purposes with each other. Co-hostile. Who could begin to fathom the slights and injustices, inflicted and borne, steadily accumulating over 68 years? How could one reckon the tally? Is there a final summation to be had? A final judgment based on where the Balance of Justice tilts, and by how much? By the tilting scales, would we be able to definitively pronounce one of these brothers Guilty, the other Innocent? Not likely.

Acknowledgements

The authors would like to thank a number of people who helped us document this story. Chief among these are Amelia Budd and her mother, Robin Emmens, niece and sister, and Conni Riley, widow, of the late Tom Emmens, for generous access to Tom's stash of memorabilia, and period photographs, the near-entirety of our photo gallery.

We are grateful to Martin D'Alexander for critiquing our manuscript and offering thoughtful, pointed advice. Furthermore, Lindsey Streitz has been a formidable help in organizing the pieces, the raw materials, into the finished product you hold in your hands. Much obliged, Lindsey.

We'd thank the contributors, but that'd be patting each other on the back, wouldn't it?

Drawing by Chanren.

From l, Pollo, Double T, Geary (in helmet), Quarrel holding Luke, Doris, Gina, Yowie, Lindy, Jay, Dana, Chaz, John R., Gagutz, Stan, Phillipa, Joy, Chanren holding Karisma. Circa Autumn '69.

Chanren holding Karisma, Gagutz looking on, 1970.

Malcolm & Mudra Simpson

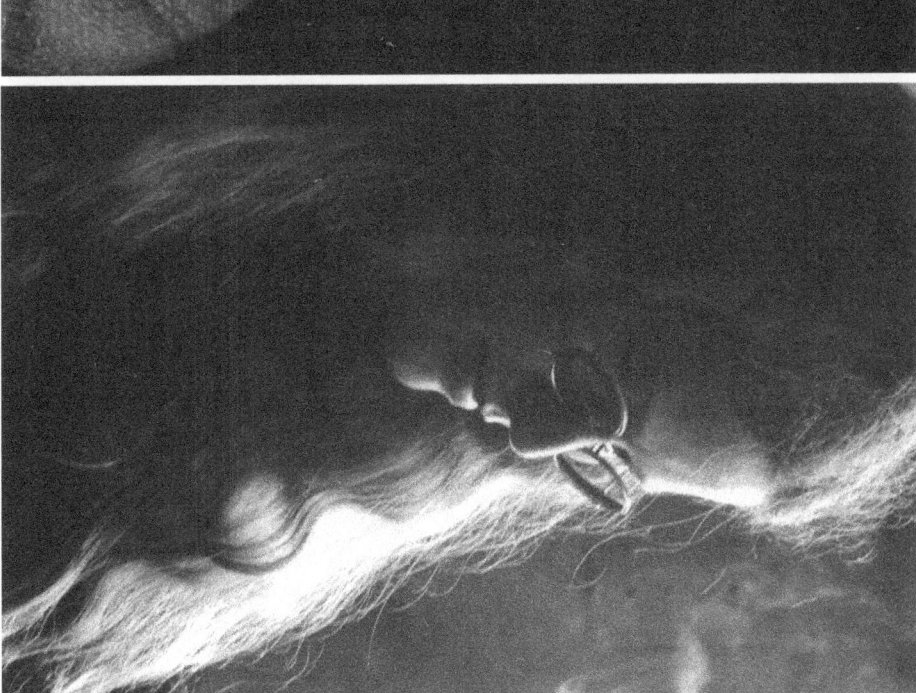

James & son Jeffrey

Dana

21. Martin Prechtel, "Secrets of the Talking Jaguar; Memoirs From the Living Heart of a Mayan Village," Putnam Inc., New York, 1999.

22. Gary Snyder, "Earth House Hold; Technical Notes & Queries To Fellow Dharma Revolutionaries," New Directions, N.Y., 1957.

23. Elizabeth Wilson, "Bohemians, The Glamorous Outcasts," Rutgers Univ. Press, New Jersey, 2000.

24. Jerome Rothenberg, "Maria Sabina-Selections," Univ. Of California Press, Berkeley, 2003.

25. Hakim Bey, "Temporary Autonomous Zone; Ontological Anarchy, Poetic Terrorism," Autonomedia, Brooklyn, N.Y. Anti-copyright 1985.R

Footnote Sources

1. Wade Davis. <u>The Wayfinders</u>, p.60
2. Joyce Cary. <u>The Horse's Mouth</u>
3. Herbert Fingarette. <u>Following the One Thread of the Analects</u>.
4. Kropotkin, Peter. "Mutual Aid."
5. June Rose. <u>Modigliani, the Pure Bohemian</u>, p.192
6. Ann Douglas. "Punching a Hole in the Big Lie," in <u>Word Virus, The</u>
7. <u>William S. Burroughs Reader</u>, 1998.
8. Wovoka, "Ghost Dance," 1880.
9. Morris Berman. <u>The Twilight of American Culture</u>, 2000.
10. Martin Prechtel, "Secrets of the Talking Jaguar," Putnam Inc., New York, 1999.
11. Roland Barthes, "Mythologies," Hill and Wang, New York, 1957.
12. Elizabeth Wilson. <u>The Bohemians: the Glamorous Outcasts</u>. Rutgers U. Press, p.25.
13. Jack Kerouac. <u>On the Road</u>, Viking Press, New York, 1955.
14. Allen Ginsberg. <u>Howl</u>. New Directions, San Francsco, California, 1955.
15. Lew Welch, "Ring of Bone," Grey Fox Press, San Francisco, 1960.
16. Alex Trocchi, "The Invisible Insurrection of a Million Minds," Project Sigma, Polygon, Edinbrough, 1991.
17. Christopher Gray, "Leaving the 20th Century," London, 1974.
18. Emmett Grogan. "<u>Ringolevio: A Life Played for Keeps</u>", Wm. Heinemann, London, 1974.
19. Sadie Plant, "The Situationist International; A Case of Spectacular Neglect," from Radical Philosophy, London, 1990.
20. Jean Barrot, "Critique of the Situationist International," Red Eye, Berkeley, 1979.

Chanren lighting up Malcolm. Autumn '68.

backs and feet—dark, mellowed hardwood—leather cushioned—each with a different size, arc and feel to it. There must have been candles, but basically the room was pretty dark. I remember going outside in the back, beneath a huge maple tree. I stood for a long time gazing up through all these branches into the explosively glistening night sky. When the smaller branches became wriggling writhing snakes and smaller worms, I went back inside.

Later a message came from Ernie, Cleda's husband, that it was getting late and somehow it was decided that Tom and I would depart. We moved to the livingroom where Cleda's peacock tapestry hanging over the fireplace mantel caught our attention. The deeply rich fabric and undulating colors were hard to extract oneself from, but we managed to negotiate to Tumor's car and through a certain force of habit, he drove a few backroads in Glenwood and we stopped at the all-night Denny's beside the freeway. We entered a world of amazing accouterments of semi-phony- American pseudo-iconic ritualistic-advertisements and other cultural mumbo jumbo. Extremely bright, the booths were all plastic and luckily not many patrons were present. The menus were encased in plastic and I had the definite impression that our waitress was also encased in plastic. She seemed like a mass of semi-liquid flesh inside a moveable plastic envelope.

What on earth could I possibly choose to order? Was I hungry? Thirsty? I think I said, "I'll have the same."

When the steaming coffee arrived and I managed to get it to my mouth, the taste sensation exploded with flavor in all directions. There wasn't much to say and I could barely keep from uncontrollable laughter. But the coffee must have had a modulating effect because I don't remember much after that.

That was my experience of Jack Ladd's Purple Domes. Buddha said as he entered the stillness, "Everything put together, comes apart."

matters; it's how much you can digest. It's not how much truth you can see, it's how much truth you can integrate into your life.'

...Where the shadows, run from themselves...
"White Room," Cream

The prevailing societal attitude was that if you discussed, or admitted the use of psychedelics, you were automatically prescribing them for others, as Timothy Leary had so vocally done. LSD became illegal in the U.S. in Oct. 1968. My own belief is that mass-medicating is a bad idea. And yet there's

The scream of the butterfly...
The Doors

The screaming in my left ear stopped- or changed- suddenly...I hadn't known it was there until that. There must have been incense burning wafting aromatic smoke throughout the room as we slowly came on. After a long pregnant silence I became aware of a sensation not unlike having to go to the bathroom. Remembering from a past circumstance the vague danger of ignoring such sensations, I thought I could traverse the distance out the door and into the next room. Once there I noticed the cacophony of movement. The light seemed like it was coming from a 15 watt bulb, yet armies of microbes were perceivably progressing across the sink counter in all directions. Then I looked up to see the mirror. It reminded me of the first time I saw television and all I could make out were patterns of dots—yet this was in ultra Technicolor. When these moving shapes finally coalesced into areas of flesh and hair, my wildly dilated eyes were noticeably beaming at me. Then areas started disaggregating around the periphery of my face. So I moved, sending shapes, lights and shadows scurrying off in many directions.

Cleda had these three old rocking chairs...intricately carved arm-rests, force has diminished."23

Terance McKenna later said, "Shamanism without psychedelics is like wife beating without alcohol, it just doesn't happen."

> *...The trees are drawing me near*
> *I've got find out why*
> *The gentle voices I hear*
> *Explain it all with a sigh...*
>
> **Tuesday Afternoon, Moody Blues**

So it was that I found myself on that hillside canyon in that funky palapa listening to those two guitar players laying in hammocks freely jamming in a light hearted way on that fateful afternoon in July (1967) in the magic mushroom mountains of southern Mexico unfettered, in accord with circumstance, just old enough to be new. The fellow I walked beside was telling me to take the mushrooms at night. I asked why. "Because," he explained, "the energy accumulates behind your knees and makes you feel like moving around in the day." Rumi says, "The way goes in."

> *...The summer had inhaled and held its breath too long...*
> *Through an open window where no curtain hung,*
> *I saw you....*
>
> *I Saw You,* **Jefferson Airplane**

"Psychedelics opened me up to an enormous range of archetypical experiences, shamanistic experiences, visionary experiences, even genuine experiences of transcendence...The tricky part was embodying these realizations." ("Wise Heart"- Jack Kornfield- Shambala Sun- 11/10)

Or as we used to say, 'It's not how much peyote you can eat that

Wasson (both from Harvard) spent most of the summer in Kansas participating in peyote rituals with the Kiowa Indians. This led Shultes to explore South America for unnamed plant species, many of them psychoactive. Wasson went to Mexico and met Maria Sabina in Huatuala de Jimanez who taught him the ways of psilocybin mushrooms. These lessons returned to Harvard and were not lost on certain members of the Psychology Department, such as Timothy Leary (later to be termed, "saint" or "the deification of psychosis," depending on one's perspective), Richard Alpert (aka Ram Dass) and Ralph Metzner, and not lost on the undergraduates such as Andrew Weil, either. When the experiments that were being conducted with Albert Hoffman's discovery (LSD-25) became well known, these same 'initiates' were primed to spread the good news. Acid..."delivered the illusion that life was an illusion as a sort of revelatory artifact," as Mark Christensen puts it in "Acid Christ: Ken Kesey, LSD, and The Politics of Ecstasy." Stanley Owsley (the "Poncho Villa of the test tube") later made some of the best acid out west.

The shaman, Marina Sabina, who first introduced Wasson to psychedelic mushrooms, described this industrialized cooptation of mushrooms from her people's point of view:

"Sometime later I knew that the mushrooms were like God. That they gave wisdom, that they cured illnesses, and that our people, since a long time ago, had eaten them... The mushrooms give me the power of universal contemplation. I can see from the origin. I can arrive where the world is born...

Before (Gordon) Wasson nobody took the mushrooms only to find God. The little mushrooms were always taken for the sick to get well... But from the moment the foreigners arrived to search for God; the 'saint children' lost their purity. They lost their force; they spoiled them. Before Wasson, I felt that the 'saint children' elevated me, I don't feel like that anymore. The my goal on self-realization. Didn't know at that point how one was to go about getting there. But I met a fellow named Russ Taylor standing in chow line at the Green Giant Pea Cannery of Waitsburg, Washington in the summer of '63 who told me about Lawson's Cactus Garden of San Antone. They would send out, for a mere $5, about 40 peyote plants, ready to plant, or dry, or eat. I ordered some.

When they arrived I believe I wrapped up a few and gave them to Yowie for Christmas. Father had to explain what peyote was to Mom. This cactus was still legal in the state of Arizona; the lawmaker crafting the bill to outlaw it had incorrectly spelled peyote with an 'i.'

As I wasn't making great headway toward self-realization on my own, I allowed that I'd consume some of the delicious cacti in my possession and see what occurred. I had done my homework, read Hesse, and had the spiritual underpinnings of "The Tao Te Ching," and other 'scriptures,' which Ken Kesey later said, "give you stars to sail by. And without those stars… a lot of people are lost." So I ate them and attempted to walk around Tucson. But the first passerby sent me into paroxysms of uncontrollable laughter. I was doubled up beside the sidewalk laughing my head off when I realized I should not be out in polite society, that this was a private quest.

The following year Anita and I went to Europe for about eight months. There was some staying with my folks in Frankfort, Germany; there was some traveling with them to Greece where we spent Christmas & New Years with Yowie. Later, we rented a little house with Yowie on a Greek Island, Siphnos, for a month. There was more traveling. In Granada, Anita and I stayed at the recommended 'backpackers' hostel and there I hit it off with a fellow traveler immediately. Amid long discussions about Gurdjieff and Buber, he shared a couple of contact names and addresses in the US where I could score some acid.

In the late 1930s the genius botanist, Richard Evans Shultes and Gordon take for granted that you approve of their actions. Silence equals compliance. Because of this ambiguous and duplicitous structure of government, responsible citizenship relies on an informed constituency beyond most folk's ability. Because of the 'lie of silence' many of us had taken up silent vigils outside various federal buildings in our cities of residence. There was a whole spectrum of reactions, but the gist from those willing to discuss the issue was that we couldn't just be 'against' something without being 'for' something else. We stood for peace.

There's an old saying that "when the mode of the music changes, the walls of the city shake." We thought that once we showed how the nightmare worked, everyone would wake up. The quest was for a formula, a silver bullet, a magic charm that would disperse the evil spell. But, of course, there is a whole jungle of silent bureaucratic and administrative outgrowths which impede and eventually strangle any opposing ideas. Elizabeth Wilson says,
The privileged class will try to co-opt these challenges by incorporating the rhetoric of the discontented… which will give the illusion that serious changes are underway, when in fact, the essential relations of wealth to power remain the same."22

We had a lot of living to do before we brought into consciousness what Gustav Landauer said: "The State is not something which can be destroyed by a revolution, but is a condition, a certain relationship between human beings, a mode of human behavior; we destroy it by contracting other relationships, by behaving differently."23

I don't mean to say that these ideas were conscious in our minds at the time we set about to manifest 'the commune', but that these expressions do now articulate some of our most deeply felt intuitions concerning what we were living through.

My mother was frequently telling me to set my goals high. So I set have failed and new ideas - including intentional extended 'family' units- were countenanced. Our revolutionary response became a kind of decentralized, leaderless movement of small communities. We wanted to transform social relations directly, through communal living, family, and work. Martin Pretchel has captured much of our thinking: a commune, he says,

is made of beautiful failures and the fruit of daily struggle... though it is rooted in this (narrative) it's people's enduring beauty feed an entangled spiritual immensity beyond the wants and needs of people.20

As Gary Snyder understands it, communal life offers a situation where the alteration of family structure can project
...a different love-and-property outlook through a whole culture (creating) groups who live by mutual illumination...a new form of family as part of the divine ecology...a synthesis of Gandhian 'village anarchism' and I.W.W. syndicalism...proposing personal responsibilities rather than abstract centralized government & advertising-agency-plus-Mafia-type-international brainwashing corporations...(This) community style of life, with an ecstatically positive vision...is opposed for very fundamental reasons to the civilization establishment.... **Today these (new) values seem almost biologically essential to the survival of humanity.21**

Baby-boomers coming into majority could see some of the social injustices of our society and responded to a few of the most offensive. That the Viet Nam war was the most immoral in recent history could be clearly seen and in turn might be demonstrated to others. I learned from discussions with members of The Resistance to The Viet Nam War what was referred to as the 'lie of silence": the power structure of the US government is set up in such a way that the leaders assume if you don't directly tell them otherwise, they is often symbolic:

> [I]t can create, at one and the same time, products and a vision of the world. The fetishism of commodities is merely the form taken by this symbolism in societies dominated by market exchange.18

As Jean Barrot says, "capitalism produces a fragmented vision of reality. But to the extent that Capitalism comes to dominate the whole of life, this vision…is inadequate to its complexity. Loneliness, stress, anxiety and aimlessness replace earlier centuries' struggle for material survival. Contemporary society isn't suffering from a shortage of consumer goods, but from a poverty of everyday life. To be rich today is to possess the largest number of poor objects.19

Sadie Plant, among others, describes the age we presently live in as an age of spectacle, "A one-way transmission of experience, a form of communication to which one side, the audience, can never reply. Mass-society-consumer capitalism is simply the society of the spectacle. The passivity and disengagement offered by modern society is a form of pseudo-participation where only the appearance of involvement is maintained."18

However, spectacle is reactive and has little to do with sophistication or subtlety. As Jean Barrot says, "the false asserts itself through its practice, by the use which it makes of the truth…Television does not indoctrinate, but inscribes itself into the mode of a being."19

The Yellow Sub was born during a period of disunity and strife: civil rights struggles, increasing opposition to the illegitimate war in Viet Nam, and the growing recognition that the government had lied to us about marijuana, the war, and who knew what else? Conventional wisdom might be seen to (what had been referred up to that time as) 'race records' to be sold to white American youth- where the real potential market was (with disposable income vis a vis allowances) in this productive, prosperous nation. Rock and Roll was so powerful, in fact, that a mere three years later it had been marginalized and merchandised: Elvis drafted into the Army, Little Richard evangelicized, James Brown and Brother Ray Charles hooked, Chuck Berry jailed, Jerry Lee Lewis deported, and Buddy Holly dead. Fats Domino continued. But teenagers could buy new versions of Tommy Sands: Jimmy Clanton, Bobby Rydell, Tab Hunter, Frankie Avalon, Tommy Roe, Johnny Tillotson, Fabian, Bobby Vee, and who could forget Debbie Reynolds? Vapid bubble-gum 'soft' rock (yawn!) overproduced, under-talented, and marketed relentlessly. That music gave me the heebee-jeebies. This didn't change, with a few exceptions, until a host of creative talents from Great Britain, responding to the original surge of breakthroughs, returned to the sources and made the music their own. It was labeled "The British Invasion". Yet rock and roll became more policed than any previous art form in history.

In 1969 Jimi Hendrix, played "The Star Spangled Banner" on a white guitar with his teeth to a half million spectators. It was the last morning of the Woodstock Festival. That was a 'Happening' (in the Alan Kaprow sense of the word) in itself. Still you could buy the record or see the movie. Nothing can withstand modern capitalism. As Christopher Grey says, "any work of art could be digested by modern capitalism.... The question is whether it is possible to create anything in contemporary society strong enough to withstand the massive pressures brought upon it."16

Industrial capitalism interposes itself between natural sources and people, selling as a commodity what previously had been freely available, water and air and many basic material needs. In casting about for a way to keep expanding, it seizes on the commoditization of experience. Take Disneyland, where 'fun' is manufactured and marketed. Sadie Plant says that such activity first time in the wake of the Second World War.

Later, Pop artists brought about a cultural understanding that popular culture was the stuff of art. Then a movement in the US gained traction to take art out of the museum and into the streets of people's lives. Alan Kaprow, for instance, was instrumental in creating 'Happenings," or participatory art forms. Art could no longer be tied to the page, canvas, or dance floor, but would reflect reality, life itself the new art. As Alex Trocchi said, "we envision a situation in which life is continually renewed by art, a situation constructed by the imagination." Imagination itself "should be applied directly to the transformation of reality itself, not to the symbols in the form of philosophy, literature, painting, etc."15

I had a showing of my art at the New World Coffee House. The principle piece was a table-top sized cut of plywood covered with red and white checkered contact paper. Fastened to this surface were four plastic plates holding plastic service-ware, catsup in packets, and local fast-food hot dogs and French fries all preserved beneath a thick coating of polyester resin glued to the surface. Later there appeared another expression of "food as art" in the dining room of the Sub: an over-baked loaf of bread nailed to the wall with a large spike. But even those were too official; in time I moved on to disposable art, like cards and letters to friends.

But--probably more than with any other cultural form, we emerged out of and were influenced by the advent of Rock and Roll which hit with such dynamic energy in the mid-1950s that it captured our attention like nothing else had. Just like Woody Guthrie writing "This Land is Your Land" in response to Kate Smith's rendition of "God Bless America," Little Richard seemed to be belting out "Good Golly Miss Molly" in response to Pat Bonne's version of "Money Honey." Elvis Presley covered Arthur Cruddup's "My Baby Left Me" as a credible improvement instead of a soul-less wash-out. When Elvis crossed over to popular music the doors were flung wide open for

Ginsburg taught us that it wasn't homosexuality, nudity, drugs or casual sex between consenting adults that was obscene. It was invasive wars, poverty, the prevention of people of color from realizing their rights as citizens and the atomic bomb that were obscene. The later Beat poet Lew Welch also sketched the condition of modern life in equally grotesque and brutal terms:

"...Driving back I saw Chicago rising in its gasses and I
   Knew again that never will the
Man be made to stand against this pitiless unparalleled
   Monstrosity. It
Snuffles on the beach of its Great Lake. Like a
   Blind, red, rhinoceros.
It's already running us down.
   You can't fix it. You can't make it go away.
I don't know what you're going to do about it. I'm just
   Going to walk away from it. Maybe
A small part of it will die if I'm not around
   Feeding it anymore."[14]

Walk away from it he did. In 1971, he left behind a suicide note at Gary Snyder's house, walked into the high Sierra and was never seen or heard from again—officially, though rumors circulated for a while that he was still alive.

   If you want to know where the Beats came from, read Thomas Wolfe, Marcel Proust, James Joyce, William Blake, Walt Whitman, Jean Genet, and Baudelaire, then set those internalized influences down on a street corner in the middle of the big city in the half-time of the 20th century with the sound of jazz that was transforming from Be-Bop to Cool, and the sight of Abstract Expressionism--uniquely American art forms--being taken seriously for the

the hoboes… Kerouac embodies these disenfranchised in swashbuckling and heroic terms in <u>On the Road:</u>

> We wandered around carrying bundles of rags in the narrow romantic streets, Everyone looked like a broken down movie extra, a weathered starlet, disenchanted stunt-man, midget auto-racers, poignant California characters with their end-of-the-continent sadness, handsome, decadent, Cassanova-ish men, puffy-eyed motel blondes, hustlers, pimps, whores, masseurs, bellhops-a lemon lot… the essential strain of the basic primitive, wailing humanity that stretches in a belt around the equatorial belly of the world…they knew who was the father and who was the son of antique life on earth.[12]

If Kerouac were extravagant in colorizing and romanticizing the marginal and outcast (he was), Allen Ginsberg exposed the opposed extreme of social and economic conditions of America's downtrodden with equal though brutal extravagance:

> Moloch whose mind is pure machinery!
> Moloch whose blood is running money!
> Moloch whose fingers are ten armies!
> Moloch whose breast is a cannibal dynamo!
> Moloch whose ear is a smoking tomb,
> whose eyes are a thousand blind windows,
> whose factories dream and croak in the fog,
> whose smokestacks and antennae crown the cities.[13]

In medieval society art had been integrated into social institutions. By the seventeenth century, however, the development of patronage began to separate the fine arts from other crafts. In France after the revolution of 1789, even these structures of support for art were destroyed. With increasing industrialization, market relations replaced patronage. Industrial economy showered populations with goods and experiences they had never known they wanted. Culture was becoming a commodity.

The ability of mass production to create new forms of art and to replace the crafts-person with the machine created conflict about the role of both art and artists. As Roland Barthes has said, "in modern society myth arises as the imaginary solution of a problem or conflict society cannot solve. Its function is to reconcile impossibilities."10 The bohemian myth attempted to resolve the conflict between artistic authenticity and social acceptance.

Bohemians were heroes to many of the culturally disgusted. Elizabeth Wilson says that "by the early years of the 20th century the role of the artist was no longer primarily to make art. Rather the artist became a figure whose role was to explore marginal states of being and consciousness. If the artist could play this role in exploring the parameters of identity then he was once more a privileged and even shamanic character."11 Art no longer needed to be a record of past sensations made by specialists manifesting objects that enslave us. In addition to realizing a work externally, art became a process of realizing ourselves as works. In this endeavor we encouraged everyone.

The Beat Generation of the 1940s and 50s was tremendously influential to us. Partially through the influence of the Beats, we also learned from the existentialists. The Beats explicitly referred to existentialism as a source of inspiration, particularly artistic expressions grounded in concrete lived experience. Critics cite existentialist writers such as Camus and Sartre, but J.D. Salinger, J.P. Donleavy, and e e cummings were also important. The Beat writers often identified with the impoverished, the homeless, the downtrodden, a life conditioned by concessions to an unsustainable, dysfunctional model of society and what it means to be human; hood-winked by convenience, worried about the opinions of others, conned by the comfort of 'well-adjusted respectability,' and so with the indifference of those at the very top of the food chain retreated from the edge where change happens. Maybe they thought that Dylan was making some kind of cryptic spiritual reference out on the edge of believability instead of telling us about concrete lived experience when he sang:

He who is not busy being born is busy dying
It's Alright Ma, I'm Only Bleeding, **Bob Dylan**

Putting it All Together

To a large extent, the Yellow Sub was bohemian. The term has long signified the artist's ambiguously marginal status. 'Bohemian,' in France, had been the traditional term for gypsies because they were thought to have come from Bohemia. In the American imagination of the '60s, people in communes were often considered to have come from a cross between gypsies and zombies.

In the Sub, we acted out an 'artistic' way of life, crossing boundaries and challenging conventional definitions. It is not so much that we lived the lives of artists, but that our lives were our works of art. In this we joined in spirit artists and bohemians all the way back to the French Revolution. It is a truism that Oscar Wilde, for instance, put his genius into his life and only his talent into his work.

as a time of day-glo, tie-dye, flower-power, "turn on, tune in, drop out," sex, drugs, rock and roll, following ones bliss, peace, love, & granola. Of course this kind of belittling compartmentalization comes from a culture devolved to bumper sticker & sound byte sloganeering. In truth, our intentional community was a radical democratic modeling of the world we wanted our children to inherit. It was the way we inhabited our lives day by day the best we could. This was not a counter-culture so much as a mythic-culture inhabiting new possibilities, balancing the political, aesthetic and spiritual. Who cared if we arrived at the spiritual through the liberal use of euphorics and psychedelics, or "head drugs," as opposed to the "body drugs": amphetamines, opiates, & most pharmaceuticals. Remember what the dormouse said in Jefferson Airplane's "White Rabbit": 'Feed your head.' We were exploring the politics of conscious liberation.

I don't mean to look back at those times uncritically. The life we constructed was not so much a response to the dominant society as a pro-active engagement with our unique life circumstances. This creative engagement with the shape of one's life is so rare as to border on never. I think our very originality underlies much of the gratuitous criticism we have received. We didn't even know whether we might be living so differently permanently or only temporarily. Most days it felt like a mixture of both.

When do you choose stability and when do you choose change? When do you seek the center and when do you seek the edge? Where is the balance? In too many contemporary American institutions, force is the primary language. Against such trends, it is essential to raise your active voice and express the truth of your principles.

Some of us were more linked to the way our parents did things. Some of us couldn't sustain the vision—maybe didn't renew it as best we might have—or maybe never had that vision so clearly etched on their souls as others did. They began to contract, shrink their minds and in consequence settled for not really possible to enter into dreams like this while the media is constantly feeding us their commodified visions, which may in fact be fulfilling the Native American prophecy that "The buffalo will rise from the ground and trample the white man to death in their dreams."7 Dreams and visions, although transitory are worth staying in touch with.

> **...Stars fell over Alabama, and I saw each star.**
> **You're walking in dreams, whoever you are...**
> ***Cross the Green Mountains,*** **Bob Dylan**

My father used to say, "Take what you want in life, but be prepared to pay for it." We took what we wanted during those years, and in the time since have had to endure many accounts denigrating that time of changes. Morris Berman, for instance, says, "in many ways the events of the sixties were an attempt on the part of the unconscious and instinctive part of the mind to assert the values of naturalness and spontaneity... but despite the reaction to the sixties, what is left over from that period of rebellion is a widespread refusal to grow up: infantilism as ideology."8 It takes time to realize that freedom requires responsibility and maintenance, and balance. "To be set free is not the same as knowing how to live free," Martin Pretchel has told us.9 Freedom is an art.

To name our experiment in intentional community as an "alternative" or as a "sub-culture" implies that the status quo is permanent. Many limited-liability-trans-national-corporations, 'bankateers,' and people who make money from other's suffering would have us believe that the market economy is fixed, natural, and eternal. Yet our present society of the spectacle is finite. On the other hand, referring to our experiment as a 'life-style' meant that our lives had some style to them--some aspects of our choosing. Chief among these was our decision to live together. Superficially it has been seen by many like Berman

Draft Information Center on the Univ. of Oregon Campus counseled people. There was The Growers Market, Sundance, and Starflower (a workers owned collective). The Kiva and Scarborough Faire provided for our basic needs. Bill Wooten of Odyssey Coffee House ran for County Commissioner and David Gwyther of Koobdooga Book Store ran for Eugene City Counselor. It was a time to be alive.

In our ongoing experiment at the Sub, a handful of folks did most of the maintenance chores and a few were slackers, doing the minimum required. Most of the crew, however, did the minimum some of the time and made extra efforts some of the time. There was also a goodly measure of gender equity manifested. I think one of the main reasons we made the impact that we did during this time at this place, is the very fact that most of us came from the southwest, and weren't raised right here in the 'Emerald Empire.' That gave us a certain subtle foreigner's mystique and some of us wielded that to our advantage.

It was also a time for dreaming new dreams. A hundred years before "Ruby Tuesday," A. Modigliani believed, that "your real duty is to save your dream."5 Dreams are our lifelines to space, a way of remembering what has not yet happened. Suppose we had a vision to silence the 'war lords'? As Edmond Burke pointed out long ago, "Authority and obedience are too fragile a bond to hold social order together for very long. We may fear the law but we do not love it...Once we abandon the public for the private, there is scant reason why we should value law over force." Suppose we envisioned a more proper place for humans in the ecosystem? Perhaps pollution is an apt metaphor for our 'industrial world.' What if we envisioned a de-mythologizing of technology? Imagine a nation where the 'Magi" rule, a 'Magi-Nation.' Can we envision a low-energy, localized abundant future? As Ann Douglas says, "in 'The Western Lands' William Burroughs imagined a new kind of currency, underwritten not by gold or silver but by moral virtues and psychological achievements."6 It's move together to the McKenzie River amid acres of cornfields, house-sitting for Bill & Peggy Brevoort who went to an ashram in British Columbia for a year.

The number of communes around the Eugene area had grown: there was the Funny Farm in Eugene; Mirkwood in Veneta; Cro Farm in Crow; Kesey's Pranksters in Pleasant Hill; and, a commune in Drain. There were others besides these as well. Lots of people felt the need to band together. We were participating in what Kropotkin calls a "biological drive to mutual aid." We had interactions with many of the other tribes, forming new alliances with affinity groups in a kind of horizontal pattern of kinship. Marty Bonnet moved in with us from a collective/commune known as the "Eugene Collation Against the War in Viet Nam." Frimpton and Joy came to us from Black Bear commune. The most impressive example of this interaction was "The Green Lakes Gathering" in the Three Sisters Wilderness Area east of Eugene. We attended as a tribe as did other communes in the area. It fostered a marvelous feeling assembling with so many like–minded participants. Bill and I spent the night eating peyote and sitting on a ridge watching the nearby mountains shoot off energy. If my memory serves, it was the first "Rainbow Gathering," although it was not called that at the time.

In the spirit of mutual aid so widespread at that time, a number of cooperatives were springing up. Besides the Willamette People's Food Coop, there was a community switchboard set up at the Odyssey Coffee House. Community gardens were getting their start. The Whitebird Medical Clinic took care of us; there was a People's Garage and the Giant Zucchini where folks could get an inexpensive meal. There was a wood coop for people who couldn't afford firewood, BRING recycling was just getting started, and Blake Free College began. Some of us sank a lot of energy into the Resistance House. The FM radio station KZEL, with an album format (as opposed to top-40) came on-line. There was the Jackrabbit Press, for getting the word out. The at having what he described as, "more than his share" of peak experiences. I felt the same way. Most of my life I would have said that if I could 'make it,' anyone could. Yet the peak experiences I've encountered have arrived in such unbidden, mysterious, convoluted, unique, circumstance-dependent contexts. They are a forcefully personalized separation from my 'small-self,' and not generally universal in any sense.

I was absent when Bob Durnell of The Funny Farm led a marathon after which Yowie was moved to make most of his personal property communal—his books, records, and clothes. Others followed suit. This re-distribution of wealth worked for a short time.

Yes, Your Blueness, I mean No, Your Blueness!
Yellow Submarine movie

We had learned a crucial lesson about the importance of personal space. We began investigating prospective real estate in rural Oregon to buy. We wanted to stop paying rent, to grow a larger garden, to explore in greater depth making our own food, brewing, baking, raising animals, honeybees, orchards, vegetable gardens. What we wanted was a re-nomadization, to resume hunting and gathering on a psychic level. Eventually this is what happened to some of us. Quarrel and Doris moved to a house near the Willamette River in Eugene where they raised a big garden. Tom and Katy moved to a cheap rental near an abandoned nursery with lots of fruit trees still growing nearby. Yowie and Gina moved to the coast to become caretakers at Gull Haven for Charles and Leslie Gray. Gull-Haven was a weekend 'get away' for Eugenians which was affordable, if people brought their own linens. As I've mentioned, Anita and I had parted, and after a while I began seeing Lindy Button. She and I decided to

> **At the first flash of freedom**
> **We rushed down to the sea**
> **Standing there on freedom's shore....**
>
> **The Doors**

We made strenuous efforts to put our histories behind us and stay present with each other. I learned the healing power of staying with my feelings as an aid to staying present. I came to pay closer attention to the stories I was telling myself and to notice how they caused my body to tighten. In time I learned to 'lay my burden down.'

I think we all learned a whole lot about each other in a short amount of time. At the end of the weekend I would call the experience I had one of the 'peak experiences' of my life: when the whole world is at your feet, as old as you'll ever get... in the embrace of the 'guide," on the verge of hysterics, it was as if a page got turned and these celestial voices filled my being. It was the highest I'd ever been without mind-manifesting substances. The marathon brought us seven people very close together, saturated us with our own becoming, gave us a deep sense of common purpose, and drew in other like-minded folks.

We repeated (or tried to) the marathon experience, with similar guidelines, four or five other times, always with varying results—Yowie said that we could be successful only to the extent that we overcame our differences. Once we went to Marcola and camped out, without a guide this time, and tried to stay with it as long as we could. It rained hard so the experience was shortened. Another attempt was at the Jerry & Phillipa Thomson's house down the lane. They had joined the commune by then. We had a guide and did a variety of exercises, some rewarding, some not. There were about 25 of us at this time and not everyone wanted to break-through to the same degree, at least not in mixed company. After several more marathons, Smokey said he felt blessed practiced the Yogi Bhajan style of yoga.

> *...Hippies out to make it rich.*
> *Oh No ! Must be the season of the witch...*
> Donovan

Pollo had this quality, whenever I opened the door for him, to walk in his characteristic kicking-his-feet forward way directly down to the basement where he would rummage around among those things I had put energy into hiding, find something or other, hold it up in sight, and ask, "is this yours?" He has an uncanny ability to attract and befriend an amazing array of interesting characters; I guess that's how I met him in Tucson all those years ago. One of Pollo's more unbalanced friends came over one day as we were listening to "God Bless Tiny Tim" or was it "Dr. John- Known as The Night Tripper?" He said, "Stop reading that Gurdjieff stuff, smoke some of this, and listen: "There are people getting together and staying on each other's case for about 72 hours non-stop, without interruption. Human defense mechanisms become overtaxed at about 10-12 hours, and wonderful things happen." Although it wasn't that simple or easy, the benefits sounded worthwhile and it seemed better than 'food for the moon,' so we began our mechanisms toward making a decision. We ended up renting a place on the coast from our landlord for a weekend, and seven of us with an experienced guide commenced our first marathon. I remember Wayne Amos taking on a major role in coordinating this event.

hand, chatting and passing a joint. We gave away free samples at one of the first Oregon Country Faires (then called "Renaissance Faire" and held twice a year). People didn't know what they were getting. We had to tell them, "It's granola, try it, you'll like it." Bringing this to market coincided with Nancy's popularizing yoghurt ('with acidophilus') through Chuck and Sue Kesey at the Springfield Creamery. The timing was perfect.

It was the duty of every resident in the sub to spend the four to five hours, depending on how many joints were involved, preparing a batch of granola. Tumor would haul a 50 gallon plastic bucket of fresh granola down the hill every morning to the Willamette People's Food Coop. Later he also delivered to another few budding natural food stores: The Kiva in Scarborough Faire; Sundance Natural Foods; and The Health Food and Pool Store at the afore-mentioned Springfield Creamery. The mariner's pay was equally divided and paid our rent and utilities plus a weekly disbursement of around $12 per person.

Tumor told the story about the time reporters from Eugene's alternative weekly newspaper of the time, 'The Augur,' came to tour the commune. On their tour, they passed through our 'certified kitchen,' in the basement, where we had hauled in and hooked-up a second electric stove, with oven, which was used only for granola. There, taped to the wall, was our granola recipe. Intellectual property rights be damned! The perspicacious reporter dutifully noted down the recipe and they printed it in the next week's article about us. Well, this must have been around 1970 or later and we were slowly scattering to the four winds anyway, being pretty fed up with living in a pressure cooker. The granola business was going the way of all disorganized, under-energized efforts. But there were some enterprising folks working a bakery at the back of the Health Food and Pool Store (so named because of the elevated pool table in the middle of the store). They began producing granola from the recipe in "The Augur." They eventually evolved into the Golden Temple, where they

Night Class" found wide audiences. R. Crumb's "Zap Comics" also originated around this time.

The music during these years (1968-71) was among the most creative and varied popular music that I ever experienced. Our extended family had diverse musical tastes and interests, so everyone had lots of exposure. Some observers say that this was a particularly fruitful time due to the American response to the "British Invasion." Folk musicians and jug bands were electrifying their instruments a la Bob Dylan at the 1965 Newport Folk Festival. Rock and Roll was maturing and becoming legitimized. But for sure, psychedelics had a lot to do with it.

When I was making my living in 'the barn' in one of the side street by-ways of Eugene, I stumbled upon a large poster of Bob Dylan's head and shoulders. It was wrinkled and torn, one from those first few years when he wore huge tousled hair out to here, dark glasses, a dark coat, maybe holding the ever present cigarette. It may have been a shot of him at a news conference or something. I hung it on the wall, opposite my bed, up-side-down.

Back at the Yellow Submarine, we began making granola, which was relatively unknown in those days, if you can believe it. Now it has even become a cliché, "That's SO granola!" A number of us simply wanted to eat healthier food than the government commodity surplus we had begun receiving. Did we ever have to wiggle through the 'hoops" to qualify our extended family (of 20 or so) for those meager benefits! Doris and Smokey did yeoman's labor in those endeavors against the welfare bureaucracy.

The only recipe we knew about was in "Back to Eden" by Jethro Kloss. He directs that you make dough of the ingredients, bake it, and then crush it with a rolling pin. Needless to say ours was an altered version. At first we bought the rolled oats and wheat with the chaff still in it, because it was cheaper. I can look back on the hours 5 or 6 of us spent seated on the floor around a large garbage can lid full of rolled oats picking the chaff out by days: Successful raids on consensus reality.

When I was a kid I listened to the Lone Ranger on our family's radio in the living room and conceived of him as a sort of Robin Hood of the American western frontier. With that in mind, it so happened that one day I came into possession of some excess pot. It wasn't of particularly good quality--probably bottom leaves--but it was genuine and would do the job. I rolled a bunch of joints, which I took to the university library (that purveyor of millions of ideas). There I walked up and down the stacks (which were open to the public in those days) pulling books off the shelves at random and inserting a joint into the depths of each book: silver bullets of serendipity.

During my commune years, I adopted a macrobiotic diet, became a vegetarian, and started an herb company, East Earth Herb, importing and distributing Chinese Medicinal Herbs with Bill Brevoort and "Ginseng" Jack Varnon.

When Baba Ram Dass (The original Flibberty-Jib-Man) came through Eugene, that was me sitting in the middle of the front row. He turned me and lots of people on to the spiritual life with an American flavor: a little Zen-talk, much heart felt devotion towards the saints & sages of Asia, and yoga practice to keep the meditation vital long enough for a response, lots of interesting stories, and chanting. As a consequence, I started meditating on a daily basis and doing yoga regularly.

Marshall McLuhan had already informed us of the importance of media in changing the world. We had studied "The Realist" by Paul Krassner. "Been Down So Long It Looks Like Up To Me," by Richard Farina had made the rounds. "The Teachings of Don Juan" by Carlos Castaneda came out during this time, which opened people's minds to realities other than the all-consuming materialistic-drift-habit-ridden consciousness, and the mental clichés people take refuge in. The first "Whole Earth Catalogue" was published. "Autobiography of A Yogi," and ("St.") Stephen Gaskin's "Monday

We recognized the transitory nature of life and, so, were not attached or overly hung-up. As much as possible we lived positively, did no harm, held respect for others, passed gifts along, were inclusive and empathetic. Did we hold to these values all the time? No, but we generally tended in these directions. You could say these were our 'ethics' or 'morals', but those words were too tired to describe this dawning world. The centerless, leaderless feelings of a rising tide were infectious. Everyone who wanted to be was in on it and practically everyone had some good ideas worth acknowledging.

Magic kept happening. We'd tell each other about serendipitous occurrences and dreams that informed our lives, and we expected these blessings to keep happening. We explored subtler facets of life than we ever could have in the workaday world and communicated these ideas to others—and not only to our close friends. We tried anything that seemed like it might work, and if it didn't work so well, or had strings attached, or created resistance, dropped it and we moved on. We were riding a flood of energy and people wanted in on it. They might think you knew more than they did because you seemed to have committed your life in a fuller way than you were raised to think was possible. Just realizing some of your potentials was enough. It didn't infringe on anyone else, in fact, if anything, it inspired others to find ways to do the same in their lives. We didn't always agree, but we danced freely.

For the most part, that spirit still lives today in those of us who nurtured the light and chose not to let it be extinguished. Those of us who let the lessons of those times sink so deeply into our souls that we could revive that spirit and manifest it in a new time with a new vocabulary, contexts, articulation, and new premises corresponding to a different age with different needs.

From the beginning it was always worldwide, it was almost never us vs. them. It was peaceful-non-violent-small-scale-direct-action-compassionate-activism. It wasn't 'ends justifying means.' It was reverential towards nature-earth. It was not predatory. It was NOW. That's what it was like for me in those became a junior partner in a trucking supply company. When that fell through I started my own shop in Fairbanks, worked for 7 years, had to endure limited bankruptcy because city reamed me of all my investments. 11 years in Faibanks, spent another year on the coast, several months in the City of Ten Thousand Buddhas (where Chanren and Lindy were living), finally realizing that most of the people there cultivating their heads invariably had bigger egos than I did, which I didn't think was possible. (Howls of laughter)

Y: So you and Gale had a daughter...

G: And raised Jackie. He was four when his father shot and killed his mother (G's sister, Lark/Lisa), before shooting himself.

(At this point for reasons unknown the tape recorder stopped recording)

(Chanren Resumes...)

I had the feeling of being alive at the right time. They were golden days, and we were in top form, having done our homework and planted the right seeds. We were making it happen, or among those who were making it happen anyway. We were causing our cells to swell up—it was that kind of feeling. You didn't have to take consciousness expanding substances, or pay attention to the incredible music on the airwaves, or listen to the news of the day chronicling the civil- rights struggles or the anti-Viet Nam war sentiment; it was everywhere, in the air. There were the day-to-day hassles, anxieties, turmoils, worries about money, and love-life difficulties that accompany ordinary living at any time. But it was the glow of being tuned-in that swept us along, fed our energy, and made us aware that we were part of some changes much bigger and more dynamic that our day-to-day getting by. The ripples we made, we rested assured, went out to all like-minded ones who were open to receiving them. This understanding gave us courage to try new ways and ideas. It was the experimenting process itself.

Y: By the time I left in December of '70, it was starting to feel like a cheap rental for a lot of people, and not much cooperation, not much common activity.

G: The drugs had begun to move in. When Sammy Costas and crew moved in, they brought the heroin.

Y: That had to've been well after I left. During my time there, we kept it to pot, psychedelics, and a little booze once in a while, and stayed away from stuff that gets you in real trouble and screws up the whole scene.

G: It certainly screwed up the scene...

(Pause) Y: Is there anything else that occurs to you?

G: I thought it was a pretty remarkable experience. I always felt that you and I and Chanren, all three kinda felt the same way about it, and all three of us left to create the situation ...

Y: ...that might have made something like the Sub experience work.

G: Yeah, I think if suddenly somebody had come along, or if one of us had come on enough money to buy some property, it might have lasted years and been a completely different thing. We pretty much felt doing it month to month in a rented house, with all the comings and goings, with people not more committed than they were. We needed a piece of property to really put the energy into it. I wasn't willing to do the things that needed to be done on a piece of rented property, plus you have to deal with the landlord at every turn...

Y: Yep, I agree completely. Were you part of a group that went to check out some properties here and there? At one point we went to Walton to check out the old school house. But...

G: We didn't have any money.

Y: It was a pipe dream. Nobody had parents well heeled enough to front us the bucks. We couldn't lean on anyone, and if we'd tried to get a loan from a bank of somesuch, they would've laughed us out of the building...

What's your life been like since the Sub days?

G: After losing my leg in a logging accident, Gale and I went to Alaska where I

G: Everybody talking peace, free love, smoking a lot of pot. I hung out for about three weeks still debating whether I should head to Alaska. Then I dropped acid, and knew I wasn't going to be a redneck trucker any more.

Y: Let alone the military.

G: The military was behind me at that point.

Y: My records show that you left the Sub with Gale in Jan/Feb 1970. What were the circumstances of your leaving?

G: There were two reasons I left. One was to go down the coast to get a job. I just couldn't earn any money at the Yellow Submarine. The two (life in the Sub, and a job) just weren't compatible. I knew I could make quite a bit more money down the coast, so Gale and I left. She wanted to leave because she wanted to get me away from all the other women. Me showing all that interest, that was her primary concern.

Y: Uh huh, that makes sense.

G: My primary concern was making money (working in the woods) so we could buy land. Then, after about a year and a half I had the logging accident and lost my leg…

Y: So, do you remember any negatives about the Sub?

G: The only negative was I didn't have enough money to stay there without a job.

Y: In those days we must have been just putting together the granola economy.

G: It was just getting started. You know, Gale came back from going to Minneapolis with the granola idea and the granola recipe, and she made the first granola. Her and I
 Sold granola at the first Country Fair.

Y: Any afterthoughts? Once you had left…

G: I just wish I hadn't. If I had it to do over again, I wouldn't have. I thought it would be a continuing thing and I thought I would be involved.

I flunked the physical due to some swelling in my knees. The two permanent employees with the Guard got wind of my flunking the physical, so they both signed affidavits testifying that I was in fit shape; they'd seen me perform any number of strenuous physical activities. So they ordered a second physical exam and, wouldn't you know it, this time I passed. When I completed the exam process, they had armed guards escort my to the airport where they flew me to Ft. Lewis.

Y: Ft. Lewis! So you were hauled away…

G: Yeah. As we approached the base, they asked if anyone was prior service. I said I was, so they separated me off to a holding barracks. All the rest were first timers who got sent off to basic training. Well, as soon as people stopped paying any attention to me, I found a back door to the barracks and just walked off base, stuck my thumb out and hitched to Eugene.

They caught me two or three weeks later; this was the fall of '67. They said they were going to give me an Article 15 and send me back to boot camp as punishment for all my misdeeds. They gave me a list of things I needed to buy before heading to boot camp. I pointed out I had no money to be doing any shopping. So they issued me a pay voucher and sent me and my pay voucher—with two armed guards—to the paymaster for $35, and when my guards were busy chatting with some other guards, I hit a side exit, walked a couple of blocks to the bus station and bought a bus ticket to California.

Y: With the $35 the army had just issued you!

G: That very $35.

Y: You were a bad boy!

G: They caught me four or five months later in San Francisco. They Court-Martialed me and gave me six months in the stockade. To make a long story short, the army finally gave me a discharge—unfit for military service—and turned me loose. And that was the time I fetched up at the Yellow Submarine.

Y: Impressions?

* * * * *

Thursday morning, 9/22/11, Yowie met Geary and his girlfriend Gloria over breakfast at the Keystone Café, an old counterculture café on Fifth Street.

Y: So Geary, how'd you hear about the Yellow Submarine?

G: I didn't hear about it at all. I came to Eugene to visit my sister Lindy, and she was living there (at the commune). She picked me up at the bus station and took me there. We were in the living room talking when out of her bedroom came Doris, naked, headed for the kitchen for a glass of water. That was my introduction to the Yellow Submarine.

Y: You thought, Hmmm, this could be interesting…

G: I thought, this might be the place! I was only going to stay a night or two before heading back to Fairbanks to finish my apprenticeship.

Y: You'd been in the military…

G: I got a draft notice. So my step-father (long-haul-trucker father not supporting family adequately, thus mother's divorce and remarriage) told me with my background in transportation, he could get me in the National Guard, and he did.

Y: Ok, you're in the National Guard, 1966?

G: 1965. I did my six months of basic training and did really well there. So I came home, and the guy in charge of the National Guard was from Eugene, from a well-to-do car dealership family. They got him his standing there. Anyway, every time they had a problem with a vehicle they couldn't fix they'd call me. I think he was afraid I was gonna get his job. The resentment, and conditions got worse and worse. At a time when I had all my money tied up in a truck rebuild, my friendly National Guard boss said I would have to appear for a two-week training session, right at a critical time in my repair-investment. I told them I could appear later but not at this very time.

When I refused to go, they turned me over to the draft. As it turns out, steal wine out of there all the time."

(Titters all 'round) Y: How come he didn't bust you?

J: He didn't care; he was just a kid with an after-school job.

Y: No skin in the game.

J: Then there was the time Carissima propositioned me on my birthday. I was too stoned to know what was happnin'. Geary told me later, she practically drug me in the bedroom. I was sittin' there going, Du uuhh hh. Missed my chance.

Y: Did she take rainchecks?

A short break, then summation, Y: You know, I've thought for a long time that the adults at the commune might've done better by you young'uns. That we were just a little too involved in our own personal lives and distractions… that's hindsight, of course. Doesn't change anything now.

C: I thought it turned out good.

Y: I guess it could've been worse.

J: Yeah, like she turned out to be a heroin addict and I became a speed freak?

Y: (after a pause) It had to've been a culture shock.

C: It was a double culture shock. First, living with my mom, and then when she died, moving in with my aunt. Total lockdown. Then, moving to the commune, the doors swung open. Yea-ah, I saw sunshine again!

Y: Yeah, but from one extreme to the other. You know, winding up somewhere in the middle wouldn't've been so bad… Oh, well. So, how's your health, Candy?

C: Not good. I've got cirrhosis and bleeding ulcers.

Y: Ugh! You in a hurry, girl?

C: Nope. They've been telling me for 20 years, "you're gonna die!"

it, pay the rent and give everybody a little spending money. It was working well.

Y: It paid our expenses.

C: I remember the graffiti on the bathroom walls, like "We are the people our parents warned us against."

J: A lot of philosophy…

C: Out of great minds…

Y: Troubled minds.

J: I remember Fancy Nancy *(of yogurt fame)* used to come over and hang out at the commune, when she was just starting out making the yogurt. What a fine, bubbly woman!

Y: Yes, indeed.

J: I enjoyed her presence. I had a crush on all these women but they were all older.

Y: Ten years older, most of 'em.

J: Mostly, I was scared. Ah, but then there was Mar-Lene. I was 19 and she was 28. She looked like the R. Crumb Jewish gal drawings. Solid, big boned. Georgeous.

C: Corn fed.

J: Her and her little boy, Deck, were from Wall Street. He'd say, "Fook oaf, dude." In that funny accent. Well, when she first got there she was with her husband. He didn't last very long, then she was there with her kid, didn't have a room or anything, so I let her have my bed. (Background commentary, Y: Out of the goodness of his heart; C: Yeah, right!) I kept being nicer and nicer, and before long she let me crawl in there with her. We started sleeping together and having a good ol' time. We'd walk down to that store there at 19th and Agate; I'd steal a bottle of wine and we'd go back up and drink it and have fun in bed. I did that (shoplifting) a long time, and then years later I was in the park, and I met a kid that'd worked in the store as a stock boy. "Oh, I used to watch you scaring the hell out of me, and how upset Billy was at me for doing that to his truck.

Y: He thought you had "done that" to his truck? It wasn't about to happen?

J: Well, it shouldn't've been driven. I was just a dumb-assed kid wantin' to go to town… Another time I was walking on 19th just about to Gancy's Ice Cream and this policeman pulls up, I mean, whips right in front of me, jumps out and starts searching me. And he finds a hand-rolled tobacco cigarette. He lights up like a Christmas tree: Ahhh, what do we have here? In a flat voice, I tell him, It's tobacco. He tears it apart from both ends, sniffs it, wads it up and throws it on the ground, all red faced, before jumping in his cruiser and squealing off.

Y: What were his grounds for searching you, anyway? His "probable cause?"

J: I was a hippie.

(A rambling group discussion off topic)

Yeah, the Granola days—I used to wonder what they found in the Granola (widespread chortling). We were basically pretty clean about it; they had to come out and inspect it to give us the license…

Y: But when you think about our legitimate "kitchen" being the laundry room of the Sub. There was a "sink" but it was a huge ferro-concrete tub to dump out your laundry.

C: Um hmm, and the home-made wine up there on the shelves.

J: We built a wooden floor, pallets laid out side by side with plywood nailed to them.

Y: Didn't we build the oven up on two-by-four bracing? So we wouldn't have to bend over to look inside?

J: Yep, that's right.

Y: The whole operation was pretty tacky, this dank laundry/mud room, maybe ten by twelve feet, no window except in the back door itself, a bare light bulb hanging from a cord.

J: I thought it was so cool that they'd take that granola down to the co-ops, sell

Let It Bleed album came out. The whole commune went downstairs and sat around listening to it:

> *Ooh the storm is raging, now they're alive today*
> *If I don't get some shelter, ooh I'm gonna fade away...*

On the album liner, it says "This album should be played loud," but you didn't have to tell us.

C: When I got there the music room was upstairs.

J: I remember it was so cool that we had all those different vehicles. You could just go out and get in one, drive it to town, do what you want, and come back. Nobody ever said anything. One time I was driving that big ol' one ton Dodge Power Wagon down Summit...

Y: With duals? The big flat bed?

J: No, That's Bubba, a one-and-a-half ton. We took it to drive in movies. We'd back it into place and with mattresses and blankets, that thing had four-foot walls on three sides; it was real cozy.

C: That's how I saw Alice's Restaurant. From the back of Bubba, higher'n a kite.

J: We'd take her to those concerts at Skinner Butte Park. But I was talking about the one-ton orange Power Wagon.

C: I think that might've been Billy 'n' Cheryl's.

J: Yeah, and the block between the axle and the spring had come out. So the U-bolts were there but it was floppy. So I was going down Summit and I went to put the brakes on, that (pressure?) came back and snapped the U-bolts, and buckled the whole front end underneath that thing, and I went sliding nose first down Summit, in that great big truck. (Here Jay manages to give a fairly accurate rendition of metal scraping on asphalt.) It's amazing we didn't turn it over.

C: Good thing you were at the wheel (with just a hint of sarcasm).

J: If I hadn't've been at the wheel, it wouldn't've happened. I remember it

I put it out or let it burn. I just remember being real paranoid because of all the pot-smelling smoke.

C: Remember that chicken shit somebody brought in? For the garden, probably. Boy, that was some nasty stuff...

J: I remember one time we thought we were going to get raided. Everybody gathered up everything and took it and hid it in the barn. I never did find my hookah. It had a tuba mouthpiece, a big-long stem, with a lined jug with a hole in the side so you could put ice in it. Well, it got stashed down there in some of that moldy hay and I never saw it again...

One time, I hadn't been in the commune more'n a week or so, Chaz Thompson, the kid with real curly hair from the house down the drive that joined the commune, let's see, I was 15 and he must've been nine or ten. He got busted at school with acid. He was trying to turn me on to...he did turn me on to acid. He said, "I got busted at school for acid; maybe you should try it." First time I ever did acid, I was 15 and the guy who turned me on was eight!

Y: They actually joined the commune. Not for long, but several months anyway.

J: After they joined I remember we had one of those group...what would you call it, a blind mill, or something like that, where everybody gets blindfolded and mills about the room getting' to know other people through touch.

Y: That must have been an attempt to build a sense of trust with each other. Touchy-feely.

J: We did a bunch of those exercises but that one was the one I remember, that blindfolded touchy-feely milling was really interesting (audible snickering in background).

C: One time in one of those group sessions you and Gina were having some trouble, so they gave you pillows to beat the crap out of each other. With the pillows instead of something worse.

J: I remember when the listening room was downstairs, and the Rolling Stones' left by December.

J: You asked about the story of the rabbit…

Y: Yes-ss!

J: I had a pet rabbit, a little, black bunny rabbit. I just loved it.

Y: Where did you get?

J: I don't remember.

Y: Out of the park?

J: Maybe. I have no idea where I got it from. One of the funniest things about that rabbit was you could take a plastic bag that had pot in it, and put that bag on the floor. The rabbit would put his nose in the corner of the baggie, smelling the pot when there wasn't nothing there. He'd push that bag all over the floor, all over the house trying to get what wasn't there no more.

C: And he'd also be out on the sun roof.

J: Our dining room was an add-on to the house and it had a flat roof. You could go upstairs and there was an openable window at the south end leading out to that roof/deck.

Y, to Candy: You used to sleep out there.

C: Yeah, summertime…

J: Well, my rabbit lived up there at night. There was a little shelter for it, and stuff. One night we were all sitting around eating dinner and we heard the horrible screechin' and thumpin', I mean, it sounded like something was getting ready to come through the roof, being torn apart, which it was. It turned out there was a big owl that lived in a tree on the corner of the property, there… Make a long story short, the rabbit was gone and the owl was fat!

(Tittering, chortling) Another memory is I had this big bunch of pot stems, probably a half pound worth, so I took 'em out in the yard and lit 'em on fire. All of a sudden there was a big cloud of smoke and it stunk horrible, and I thought, Oh, my God, we're going to get busted! But I didn't want to put it out and leave some evidence; I didn't know what to do. I can't remember whether how everybody was, until the commune. Peace, love, and dope—and I mean marijuana when I say that.

C: Oh, I learned a lot there. Just like Jay, I didn't have to conform to some other person's idea of how I should be. I could have my own ideas about things, and...I could be a person.

J: I thought I caused a lot of people at the commune a lot of grief with my late night music, friends and acid trips.

Y: Maybe you did. So what?

J: Of course I didn't think about it at the time but looking back, I must've driven those poor fuckers crazy... (Living at the Sub) I did sort of neglect my education, but I don't think it would have mattered.

Y: Did you guys not go to school after you came to the Sub?

C: I went for a couple of months.

J: I did. I went for two years. I finished 9th grade at Roosevelt Jr. High and when I went to register the next school year, they said, "You're an out of district student," like I'd done something wrong, or something. Then I went to an alternative school, which I really liked, but when it got shut down, that was it for education.

Y: How old were you when you came to the Sub?

J: Fifteen. C: Twelve.

Y: So Mud must've been ten?

Both: Yep.

J: I tried calling Mud yesterday and today. He's just not answering.

Y: Well, Candy, what other impressions do you have of the commune? What was bad for you?

C: I think when things starting to break up, you guys, being the main foundation, had left and a bunch of shit-people started moving in.

J: Speed freaks and heroin addicts.

Y: Yeah, Lindy had left with Chanren in November '70, Gina by then also. I going. It was either stick with the aunt who probably had her hands full anyway, or come to this place that was probably not the best setting for little kids.

C: Ah, I thought it was great.

Y: Mud's eyes were about as big around as saucers when he first got there.

C: I remember when we first pulled up in the driveway, first thing Jay said, "Come here (Candy's voice taking on the tone of a seductress), I got something to show you." And he took us up to the music room and got us stoned.

J: That was a mistake, 'cause then you wouldn't leave me alone (chuckles all around).

Y: That took place probably within a half hour of your arrival.

C: Oh, yeah; "come on, come on…" There were all those black-light posters, the lava lamp, and stuff.

J: The commune was really a blessing for me because I was a serious racist before coming there.

Y: What do you mean? Anti-Blacks?

J: Just anyone, if you weren't white, you were a piece of shit.

C: He wasn't like that before living with our aunt.

J: Living in Oroville. Yep, I was a racist and a punk, you know, going around picking on the little kids.

C: Well, you still are. (Guffaws at Jay's expense)

J (Enduring the slings and arrow to his dignity from an unrepentant little sister, the "reward" for his candor): The commune taught me that niggers come in every color, and just because somebody's a different color don't mean he's bad, or nothing. I learned that people of every color are people.

Y: Yep. A valuable lesson, doncha think?

C: Very.

J: I was so blessed that I got rid of that horrible, hateful feeling.

Y: What a curse that is…

J: I didn't realize it 'til I lived in the commune a while. I just thought that's

J: No, not at all.

Y: Why do you suppose?

C: Pretty much on the run from the army.

Y: Lindy came to the Sub in April of '69, Geary in mid-June, and Jay in mid-August, but Geary left at the end of January '70, according to the stats I kept.

J: I don't remember Geary being there when I got there.

C: I remember Lisa (aka Lark, younger than Lindy but older than Jay) dropping by occasionally, hitch-hiking on her way to California, or someplace.

J: The first time I heard of the Yellow Submarine Commune was on the bus from Oroville to Eugene with Lindy. I was under the impression she had her own place and I'd have my own little room. After we got on the bus, she started telling me, "Oh, I live in a commune with a bunch of hippies." At this point in my life, I'd only ever seen one hippie and I didn't really know what they were; you know, I'd heard stories. So we climb out of the bus in Eugene, Oregon and there's Quarrel sittin' in that old milk van painted red, white, and blue, stars and stripes, him with a big ol' beard and glasses. Lindy sings out, "Oh, there's Quarrel!" I didn't know what to think. Ba deeba dub duuh…

Y: What am I getting into…

J: I was in shock. Then, ride in that milk truck, get out and there all these hippies. Fine, lovin' people.

Y: Chaos.

C: I remember Lindy and Katy came and got me and Mud. The first time I heard anyone say fuck out loud. We were driving up here and we had a flat tire. I remember Lindy walking around and kicking the tire, and saying fuck! I thought, I'm glad Aunt V didn't hear that.

Y: But living with your sister seemed like it would be a better deal than with your strict aunt, even if you didn't know the details of what it would be like?...

C: Yeah. Right.

Y: But you guys were little kids and didn't have much say in where you were

Jay and Candy Button interview, 9/21/2011, Geary Button the following day

It's a warm, sunny Wednesday afternoon in Jay Button's south-facing room. He and Yowell Mebsanuri begin the interview when, soon after, Candy Button joins them.

Yowell: How old were you when your mother died?

Jay: Twelve.

Y: Who did you live with before you came to the Sub?

J: I lived with my aunt and her family for three years in Oroville, California. I was a little redneck/racist/punk. Candy and Mud were there with me.

Y: Was that comfortable living with your aunt's family?

J: It was re-eea-lly hard because we'd been such hellions… to move in with my aunt who was very, very straight and religious. It was church twice on Sunday, Sunday school in the morning and service in the evening, and again Wednesday evening, going from no discipline to severe discipline… At home (with Mom) she'd work nights and sleep days. The older kids took care of the younger kids.

(Candy makes her entrance; there are hugs and greetings, reacquaintance after many years. We resume talking about life with their aunt's family.)

Y: So, your aunt had high expectations for you guys. And you guys were young, didn't have much choice in the matter.

J & C: Uh Huh

Y: Then once Lindy joined the Sub… She and Gale joined about the same time.

J: Lindy came and got me in the summer of '69 and got them in '70.

C: She had to turn 21.

J: She told us she'd come and get us as soon as she could.

Y: And Geary wasn't involved in that?

We came back to the Yello-Sub and Eugene was having a "Be-In" with live bands at Skinner's Butte Park. There we met three young women (Katy, Molly & Rita) who wanted their newly acquired puppies to be baptized. We were exactly the ministers who could do it right, and we did, there in the Willamette River with an ad-hoc, made-up ceremony. Both Molly and Katy would later become members of the Sub.

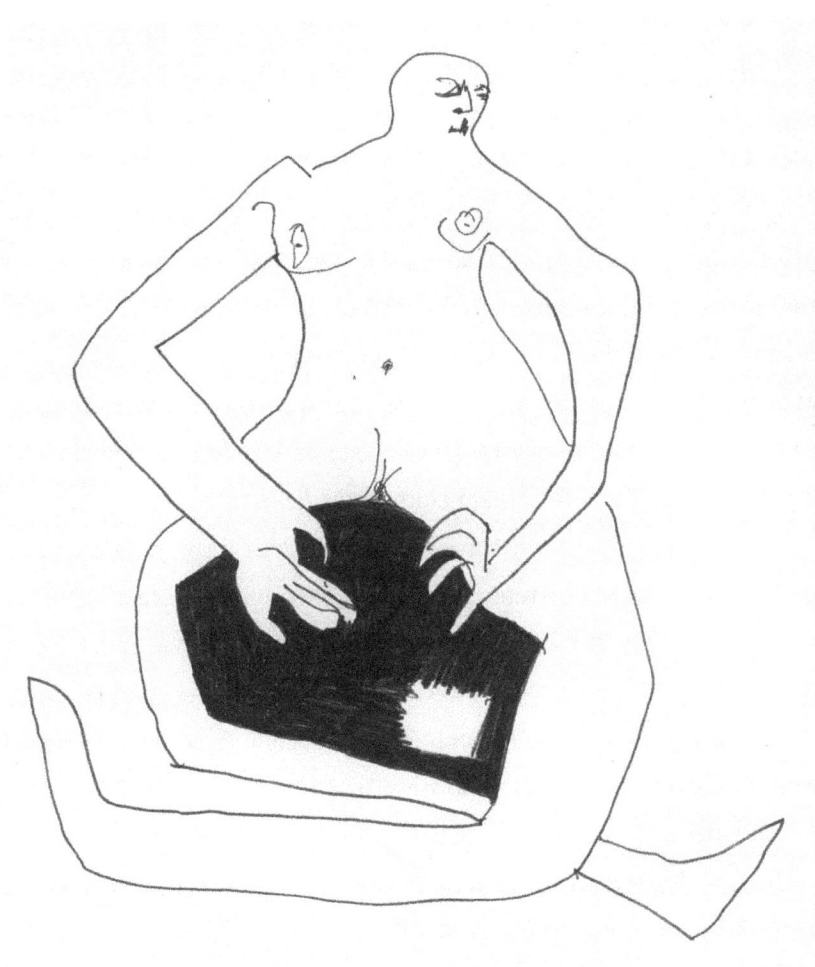

thought Zepplin was the best band ever, and overplayed them, at top volume, repeatedly. Our hosts also shared with us the little known fact that you could become a Universal Life Church Minister just for the asking. We drove right past the Universal Life Church in Modesto that following day and found the place from the address on our friends' minister certificates. To his last days Tom could recite that address from memory. I can't recall if it was an actual church or just a big house, but there in the back was a cluttered office and the Right Reverend Kirby J. Hensley who did so much for freedom of religion in this country. He expeditiously signed the three of us up on the spot and might have asked for a donation. We rolled on down the road to Flagstaff as certified ministers discussing how we could best use our new found stations in life.

In Phoenix Tom met many of our diverse circle of friends: Sonny & Nikki's family, my high school chum Verlis, and Jim Zoeckler, or "Zeke," the brilliant tenor saxophonist whose biography is inextricably intertwined with the history of modern jazz in Phoenix. We stayed with the Tracers in Tempe. Then we went to Tucson and stayed with Yowie's friends Double T and Gina and communed with Jose and Augusta, we got turned on to Traffic's second album and Credence Clearwater's first two albums. I remember smoking pot and going up on the roof to overlook Park Avenue, University nighttime traffic, and the glorious moon and brilliant stars of the desert.

On the way back we stayed in L. A. with Tumor's sister and her husband, then resumed our return trip north, through wine-tasting country. I don't remember a lot. It was my driving shift because Yowie and Tom "over-tasted." I recall singing along with the radio, "Going up the country, don't you want to go?" and, later, when my companions resumed coherence, discussing philosophy, history, psychology, politics, and a particular waitress in Pismo Beach. I've never forgotten the camaraderie established during that crucial trip to the SW. Instead of being fed-up and bored by the end, this incredible plethora of experiences created a closer bond between the three of us.

what meaning these labels will have in the future. Secondarily, as Joyce Cary says in The Horse's Mouth." The world consists entirely of exceptions."2

> *...From fixtures and forces and friends*
> *your sorrow does stem*
> *that hype you and type you*
> *making you feel like you gotta' be just like them...*
>   *To Ramona,* **Dylan**

The sense of "jen," or membership in a group or community, is described in Confucius' Analects as pervasive and profound. It implies a sort of commitment, unlike a classification, to some person. There is a sense of being committed to one's word. Confucius' concept of loyalty is distinctively oriented to the integrity of individuals, self, and others, in contrast to the emphasis in Western culture on group as object of loyalty. Human relations are conceived as relations of person to person within a communal framework. 'Jen' is a dynamic stance, described by Herbert Fingarette in "Following the One Thread of the Analects" as "THAT DIRECT, IMAGINATIVE, ANALOGIZING OF SELF WITH OTHERS THAT IS INDEPENDENT OF RULES, FORMULAS, OR GENERALIZED DESCRIPTIONS...IT IS THE STANCE-IN-ACTION OF BEING TRULY HUMANLY ENGAGED."3

Yowie, Tom & I headed south in early 1969 in Tom's tan V-dub hatchback, as usual with his camera. The first night we spent in Oakland crashing (by prior arrangement) with a couple, I'd met through dad's humanities classes at NAU. In fact I'd bought my Volkswagen van from them. While we were there, they kindly introduced us to the first album of Led Zepplin, which was later to become Tumor's bane, as some younger communards for the shelter but the entire mind-set was unpalatable to me. Somehow I was introduced to Yowie at the New World Coffee House, and got invited to join the group. I don't remember any of the exact circumstances but it was a providential turn of events for me.

I never felt that I had much of a contribution to make to the group due to my lack of maturity. There was so much I didn't understand about how to be in the world: the purpose of money, the need for avocation. Things I didn't learn until later. In spite of those limitations, I felt accepted by everyone. I wish I had been able to make more of a contribution other than stir granola and help out generally.

We had a ritual of sorts. Formulated in the waning hours of an acid trip, it was called "marking time." Late at night we assembled all the partial cans of paint around and enough brushes for each and traipsed down the lane to a place marked by an unusual amount of cracks in the roadway, which described lots of interesting various shapes. The only rule was to not paint any words, or images. Thence we set about beautifying our world with colors of house paint in all those flat shapes both large and small. I remember there being anywhere from two to a half dozen participants each time we enacted this midnight enterprise. Most of our project would be dry the next morning by the time the first resident began the drive to town from our neighborhood. Had we made their lives any brighter, more colorful? Did they even notice?

We were participatory artists, political activists, spiritual psychologists-philosophers, all of these and more, alive in our time. Calling us 'hippies' was as inane as any category-label for a group of individual people. This crutch is what cocoons and prison walls are made of. In the first place, we can't know was serious in that fear- burdened way that we should be concerned about being infiltrated, and if this were so, he was not going to be further involved. I mean there were Malcolm and Mudra working up position statements for the Revolutionary Union ("Are you R.U.?") in the back room. "What do you call communism? someone asked. But the other thing I remember about that night was coming up to Yowie who was sitting on the front porch eating, leaning over and kissing him on the forehead... unprovoked, without preamble. Just that.

There were lots of days in the early year or two when we were gifted to have remarkable visitors. One day I remember standing together on the Yellow Sub front porch were Jack Ladd, a 'genuine' warlock of highly developed power; Scott Bartlett, a noted Politico-spiritual-Agitator; Bill Brevoort the herbal visionary; and Jerry Ferrox, kingpin of the Hoedads tree planting collective & later a 20-year Lane County Commissioner. Large-as-life western characters, each one with a highly divergent personal narrative, crossing paths at this unique time on the outskirts of Eugene. Here's how member John Richey recalls it:

I had hitch-hiked to Eugene from Tallahassee in 1969 because of a woman—a fruitless endeavor, as it turned out—and found myself in a fairly desperate situation: thousands of miles from people I knew, cold, broke and lonely. I had been taken in by a born-again Christian commune that occupied a large house somewhere downtown Eugene. I didn't make any friends there during my brief stay and my strongest memory was that they served oatmeal for breakfast. Oatmeal is a peculiar food for a southern boy—I suppose because oats (wheat, barley either) don't grow much in the south. Corn is what we have, grits. At any rate they were sincere enough people and I was grateful associates. The artists that Pollo Smith knew were largely welcoming towards us. The various social interactions fostered through The New World Coffee House, where some of us worked proved fruitful.

Sometimes we acted as energizing catalysts as in the case of the small 'War Resistance' group we found in Eugene when we arrived. With the help of most of the early group, spear-headed by Malcolm and Mudra Simpson, the group became more focused and active and came to rent a house on Ferry & 12th Streets. Later our many contacts in making and distributing granola expanded our circle.

But that Resistance House was something. A large, single-story, wooden affair within walking distance of the U of O campus, it had huge windows in every room and a seventy-year-old wide porch clear across the front. It would have created lots of renter interest except that Alison Cadbury, the owner of the New World Coffee House, was vacating it and let those of us involved in the Resistance rent it after her. Did she own it? I don't know but she did in the years of her residence there commission a leading cartoon artist of Eugene, one Paul Olswang, to paint a very large fantastic mural on the living room wall.

One of the first gatherings there was an enormous potluck. By this time, Anita and I had parted, and I had, by some twist of fate, just spent a couple of hours at "The Funny Farm" commune with a young woman who 'read me' the whole album, "Music From Big Pink" with her eyes gazing into mine. No words were uttered, but I came away with a much deeper understanding than I had prior to that of this pivotal album. I was so naïve that it didn't enter my mind until sometime later that she may have wanted me to make love to her.

She came with me to the crowded potluck, where there were multitudes of sumptuous food, camaraderie, and political ferment amid friends both new and old. At one point a very influential character of those Eugene days, Franklin Ari, said in a very loud voice, "Wait, there are communists among us!" He good measure planted. But owing to its rather remote location, I think we were forgetful about watering and the effort had a pitiful outcome.

My V-dub van transformed during my years in residence. I painted the outside like an imagined current American circus wagon. On one side were blazoned images, logos, and brands of commercialism dominated finally by a six-foot long Armstrong tire rhinoceros in bright pink. The other side contained an abbreviated visual history of the circus. I had already completed an image of the Circus Maximums, traveling gypsies, portraits of P.T. Barnum and James Bailey, and the five Ringling Brothers when one of the most enigmatic occurrences of this time happened.

We parked our vehicles on a pull-out created by many loads of fill-dirt 50 yards down Floral Hill Drive from the actual house. On this pullout one day late in our history arrived a black late '50s DeSoto coupe. Where had this car come from? Who owned it? Would they be back? When? We watched it for several days before we examined it closer. The keys were in it and there were no bodies in the trunk. In fact, in the trunk were several magazines, the one on top containing the very photo of the five Ringling Brothers that I had copied in paint on the side of my van. Eventually, we ascertained that the vehicle was not stolen and began driving it.

One day Doris, Luke and Quarrel arrived from Seattle in their converted bread delivery van, freshly repainted by Tom Cherrytree. Quarrel said, "I come empty-handed."

We began to infiltrate and form a growing number of connections to people in Eugene from a number of socio-economic levels. James Livingston and I took on the task of digging a sewer hook-up ditch for the Thompsons, who lived down the hill. It was while digging this ditch that I first listened closely to Janice Joplin, with Big Brother & The Holding Company on the "Cheap Thrills" album. This was also about the time that Yowie went to work at the Diamond A Cannery and met Ton Emmens along with some of his circle of

> **We pointed you the way to go**
> **And scratched your name in sand.**
> **But you just thought it was nothing more**
> **Than a place for you to stand...**
> **Tears of Rage, The Band**

Fairly early on Pollo heard of a 'Home Comfort' wood cook stove available for the taking. A couple of his friends who had originally created 'The Daily Flash,' a head-shop on Ferry and 11th Street, had sold their business and were moving. Pollo and I went there one evening and with the help of his friends wrestled this very heavy stove into Pollo's van. Installed in the living room of the Sub, it kept us warm burning wood we could scavenge. Teen-aged Jay once tried an experiment to see how high he could get the thermometer on the oven door. I happened through late in the experiment at 900 degrees--with most of our wood supply gone. I put a stop to the process. To me that woodstove was as emblematic as anything else of the commune. I still know of its where-abouts.

Pollo built a large enough table to accommodate everyone in the ever-growing family at once. It resided in the living room for a long time, dwarfing the space, so the next summer we moved it out to the patio where it was pleasant to sit and chat.

We began gardening—finally. Our first attempt was in a rather shaded area close to the main house. We worked the soil up, without adding many nutrients, planted a variety of vegetables, and hoped for the best. I remember pleasant afternoons spent weeding there. The feel of my hands in the soil transformed me in a subtle way. The next planting season this area was the scene of the city-sewer hook-up excavation. But our gardening interest was already focused on the lower sunny part of the adjacent pasture where we had permission to try a larger garden. Some of us toiled to work up the soil, and in who arrived in the first year could rightfully be regarded as a 'founder.' It was bro Yowie who seized on the name, "Yellow Submarine." But the commune itself was highly influenced by The Band's first album, "Music From Big Pink," which had just come out, blowing everybody's mind. They'd named the album after the house where they were jamming with Bob Dylan in Woodstock, N.Y. Their house was similar to ours except that ours was yellow. There was also a popular notion at the time of a widespread underground, though mostly on the East coast. Skeptical of this claim, "the subway is not the underground," sang Country Joe & the Fish. Being on the other coast, we had a different perspective and described our project as sub-marine. The name stuck, partly at least because no one had a better suggestion.

One of the very few votes I can recollect was the one many months later over whether to change our name to 'Rivendell.' We voted in favor of the change, and as fate would have it, a few days later we were visited by people doing an article for "Mother Earth News.' That is us in that long-forgotten issue, under 'Rivendell.' The name never gained traction since we already had some name recognition among a growing network of communes, Lama in New Mexico; Drop City in Colorado; Black Bear in Northern California; Magic Mountain in Takilma, Oregon; and Kesey's Pranksters out in Pleasant Hill. The Hog Farm, with Saint Misbehavin' (Wavy Gravy) may have been going by this time.

So much for voting. Consensus was our preferred method of decision making, anyway. Any good idea could gain favor, but an idea not instantly popular required lobbying, coalition building, and lots of patience. I remember successfully lobbying a kitchen full of mariners to consider having a marathon.

those reasons, and others of course, 1969 saw us headed south again toward Phoenix and our families.

I didn't add much to the Yellow Sub, though I took a lot away with me. One of the projects while I was there was to build stairs on the back porch. I really liked the physical movement and clarity of carpentry, so in Phoenix, I began apprenticeship as a union carpenter. Later, I spent about a thousand years in college, mostly evenings and mornings until I got to grad school. I am convinced that these new directions in my life grew substantially from the self-assertion that led me to, first visit, and later, to live briefly as a submariner.

So the Sub didn't fail, for me. I formed enduring friendships, with Tom Emmens and Pollo Smith and reinforced already strong relationships with Chanren and his brother, Yowie. Most importantly for me, the political activism of the '60s changed everything, even though we are still struggling through a powerful and entrenched reactionary backlash. The active changes in civil rights, feminism, the shape of the family, and the war in Vietnam were the most significant social transformations of my lifetime, and I was in on them, thanks in large to the Sub.

(Chanren resumes)

Soon after James took up residence, he and I took to foraging in nearby Hendricks Park which we called Jimi Hendrix Park. In the park, we found abandoned plum trees, apples, and abundant wild blackberries for the picking. One afternoon James returned from the park with a prize, a baseball sized bird nest, tightly woven, on a mossy branch maybe 3 feet long, home to a somewhat small bird, but abandoned. It was the first living room decoration of note.

The commune was un-structured in such a way that almost anyone own consumption at, I think, thirty cents a pound. Wayne Amos and I picked hazelnuts at a similar bargain. In addition, a number of us were available for neighborhood projects: digging ditches, painting, roofing, and so on.

Presidential candidates were campaigning for their party's nomination that year, and one night we joined a caravan to Portland, where Hubert Humphrey was stumping for the Democratic selection. His anti-war rhetoric was too tame, and students at Blake College had duplicated invitations to one of his more-or-less select gatherings. Several dozen of us took seats on the auditorium floor and at a prepared signal we all marched out chanting, No More War! I remember that Mr. Humphrey was absolutely unruffled, saying to the remaining audience, "Well, good. Now we can get to work." I felt theatrical and childish until I remembered that the point was to convince the government that the war in Vietnam must be stopped.

A few evenings later, the painter Harold Hoy and his wife Kathy stopped by the commune to see Pollo, who was out. We talked and Harold invited me along to his studio for the evening. He was painting hard edge stuff, by hand. I modeled a weird creature from clay. He invited me to participate in his weekly paint studio at the U of Oregon. After May arrived, that class became part of our routine, along with a clutter of unaccomplished paintings in our bedroom.

Our son Jeffrey was sharing our bedroom again, for the first time since his infancy, and that lack of accommodation for children eventually became important in our leaving the commune. One of the hangers-on at the Sub, a supposed friend, began showing up when I was working or at paint class to bird-dog May. That pressured our leaving as well. Eventually, it became clear that it was not possible for us to function as a family in any way that May or I could understand. For

"I miss May."

"You know she probably won't come."

"Well, then, I'll do the next thing."

At Stockton, we stood on opposite sides of the freeway until an old Chevy pickup pulled over in front of Kim. He ran to the rear door, tossed his sleeping bag inside, then turned to wave goodbye. I looked north where there was an overpass, a service station, and a grocery store. I could buy a postcard and mail in my resignation. Beyond the overpass, beyond my vision, were the Sierra Nevadas and the Cascades. I swear I could smell the snow on Mt. Shasta.

Back in the commune, I found that the bedrooms were nearly all taken: three stories of breathless "communards," as Tom Emmens eventually dubbed us. On the attic floor lived Pollo Smith with his son Gagutz. The entry to their bedroom was via a set of dark, narrow stairs which opened off the dining/kitchen area. Pollo wore hard leather boots, and always in a hurry, thundered up or down those stairs like a wild horse breaking free.

In the very basement, lived Wayne Amos, a writer and adventurer from Kansas whose prose piece, "Listen for a Quiet Voice," had recently appeared in <u>The Reader's Digest</u>. When Wayne took up residence, the Sub was full.

Rotating shifts for evening meal preparations, with individual breakfasts and lunches: monthly food expenses were shared along with all other operating expenses, mainly rent and utilities. May did decide to bring Jeffrey and come, after all, and basic living expenses for the three of us were under thirty dollars per month. To keep communal expenses so low, we foraged, bartered, and bargain-hunted endlessly. We picked chanterelle mushrooms in Hendricks Park across the street. Chan and I had already spent part of an afternoon picking green beans for our of milling bodies we passed until I saw Kim. He fell in step beside me and began chanting. At the temple we ate a vegetarian feast using our fingers as utensils, then settled in for meditation.

Kim had been seated across the room from me when we came in, so I walked around and sat beside him. "I think I have enough money for two Lowenbraus at that market on the corner," I told him. We left the temple together and drank them standing on the sidewalk. Kim told me that Zack had sold the car and offered to buy a ticket so he could go to Hawaii with him, but he had decided to go back to school. He stopped off at the Yellow Sub where he learned that I was in San Francisco for a few days and decided to look me up.

"Are you still writing this down?" he asked.

"Yeah."

"You should write that it was your most expensive vacation ever."

"It wasn't. I still have a little money left."

"But now you're going to quit your job and move to Oregon, aren't you?"

"How could you know that?"

"I read ahead."

"You're right. I'll hitch out to Stockton with you. You can catch I-5 south, and I'll head north." We walked to the nearest freeway entrance. "Did you go see that girl in the convertible?' he asked.

"Yeah."

"Didn't you like her?"

"She's alright. I'm going to call May when I get to the Yellow Sub and see if she will come.

"You're getting homesick, aren't you?"

from then on. The best I could foresee from my desk that morning was forty years more of the same... I would come out the other end of that eternity like the grown-ups with whom I shared my office, whom my eminently tasteful reserve forbids me presently to describe.

By contrast, I could be a part of something fun and subversive. It seemed clear to me that the war in Vietnam grew partly at least out of the wars at home. Therefore, it would be necessary to change a few things here: racism, sexism, dysfunctional families, stultifying, counter-productive work, unresponsive political organizations, and unfair economic conditions. That was a job to do, and a commune seemed a good place to start to do it. I could see that a lot of people shared my ideas—were miles ahead in thinking the situation through. Where had these people been until now? Had they, like me, merely been guarding their better natures until they felt secure?

On my last morning at the Haight, I decided I would hitch to the Bay Bridge and across. By the time I reached the other side, I would know whether to head north to the commune, or south, to LA, and eventually, Phoenix. I had about enough money for one meal on the road whichever direction I took.

At the Embarcadero, a new white van pulled to the curb, a Hare Krishna singer stepped out, and fell into step beside me. We said helloes.

"Do you know where you're going?" he asked.

"Not really," I said.

"Why don't you come with us?"

The van was crowded with singers, thick with incense, and a-jingle with the sound of bells and cymbals. We were on our way to sing down along Haight and back up to temple. I felt conspicuous and insincere without a saffron robe and avoided eye contact with the blur and the faintest smattering of freckles. She was almost three months pregnant though not yet showing, and recently abandoned by her boyfriend. For the next several days she would show up at Union Square at two or so in the afternoon, I would close up my book-selling enterprise, and we would vamoose on our walking and talking tours, always starting with a quick up and back down the outside elevators at the Fairmont Hotel to begin. She would return home, across the Bay in the evenings, and I would house myself at Haight Defense.

One evening, just about time for her to head home, we were inside a Tower Records, standing as close as possible to the speakers and shivering, in the absolute precision of In a Gadda Da Vida to capture the energy of that summer. We watched a family of four thread their way through the crowded doorway into the shop, first, the father, who, inside, turned, scowled, and said something in a snarl to his wife, who followed him. Once she pushed her way inside, she turned and said something with an ugly face to her son, who looked to be about twelve. He turned almost instantly and slugged his sister, a year or two younger, on the arm. I looked at Linda, who nodded. She had seen it too. It was a small sample, but from what I could see, the violence that we were raining down on the Vietnamese was matched by the violence we visited upon one another at home.

Time was running out. In a few days, I would have to head up to Oregon or back to Phoenix to see if I could get my old job back. I remembered a morning at work, looking up from my desk at the vertical blinds which partially concealed the street outside—Main Street in Mesa—from view. From where I sat, the blinds were turned at such an angle that they seemed like prison bars. As I understood, or misunderstood, then, careers began at my age and followed that course

The flyer announced that the Steve Miller Blues Band would perform, but that possibility began to lose its luster when I arrived at the park where Panthers with banana-clip carbines were standing guard around the perimeter. I read a quotation by Eldridge Cleaver on a Free Huey poster. It said: There seems to be little hope of avoiding armed war in the streets of California and of preventing it from sweeping across the nation. If there has to be a war, then let there be a war.

I noticed, then, that there were more armed Black Panthers standing guard on the surrounding rooftops, and no Oakland cops in sight. I decided to see Steve Miller another day. On the walk back toward the city center, I passed several large recruitment posters for the Oakland Police Department. Nobody wanted to work for the cops in Oakland, I guess.

The ready possibility of violence was a shock to me. I had been raised on a liberal view of history as a progressive march toward increasing liberty and prosperity. Now, America's poor were being shepherded to Vietnam to fight a war which made no sense to anyone, including Robert McNamara, who was in charge, more or less, of the thing. Here at home we were continuing a long-undeclared war against Blacks, and the Panthers were ready to take it up a notch.

The Haight Defense Group offered literature that we could sell on the streets, a small cheaply-printed chapbook named The Hippies. The booklets cost us fifty cents each and we were advised to sell them for as much as we could get, probably between one and two dollars. I remember a militantly middle-class matron in Union Square who refused to buy a book from me (for two dollars) unless I "confessed" that I was, myself alone, an actual hippie, which I promptly did.

It was on such a selling jaunt that I met Linda, golden and young, well proportioned and athletic, with blonde hair below her shoulders was leaving for San Francisco, but that I might decide to return. He reminded me that they couldn't hold my room, but I was already facing south.

When I arrived in Oakland late the next afternoon, I called Carol, figuring that she would make it clear in a hurry that she was busy. Instead, I would hitch across the bridge to sleep on the floor at the Haight Defense Group. She answered and gave me her address, which was only a short walk from the phone booth.

We completed one another perfectly. She was happy, confident, hopeful. I wasn't. We walked and talked without energy, took a drive into the city in her convertible where we had Chinese food. I left the next morning after an uncomfortable night on a small sofa in the entry foyer. I had only three days of vacation left and a lot of questions unanswered. I hitched across the bridge once more for another round of sightseeing and had my last breakfast at Big Mike's Pool Hall. The next time I visited, Big Mike's would be defunct, its boarded windows scrawled with graffiti.

That night and for the next week, I stayed at the Haight Defense Group, an industrial-strength crash pad downstairs from the Black Panthers headquarters, which was not very active since most Panthers were either out organizing, in jail, or dodging bullets from white cops. I did pass Eldridge Cleaver now and then on the stairway.

I went to a Black Panther fund-raiser to help with Huey Newton's legal defense on a Saturday afternoon at DeFremery Park, which the Panthers were trying then to rename Bobby Hutton Park. They are still trying. Bobby Hutton was their former Treasurer, shot down in the streets of Oakland by white cops. This killing had happened earlier that year, in April, a few days after Martin Luther King was assassinated. Bobby Hutton was eighteen years old when he died.

three story yellow farm house, consisted of Chanren and his wife Anita, Chanren's brother Yowie, the writer Wayne Amos, the architect Pollo Bitmer and his son Gagutz, and me, briefly.

Chan and I drove to a farm that day to pick string beans at a few cents a pound, then prepared dinner together with Anita. We stayed up late listening to music and passing around the peaceful pipe, speaking in earnestness about historical social transformation. They were going to change work, family, history, and the future. Me, I kept thinking about my wife in Phoenix. When the last toke was toked, we slept.

At breakfast next morning I met Dorothy, a divorcee from across the road, who brought apples over and then stayed for pancakes. When we had finished eating, I fixed up my room, fluffing out my sleeping bag and stretching it across the floor at one end, leaning my backpack against the wall at the foot of the bag. Dorothy brought a Polish movie poster for me and the room started to seem really festive, if a little crowded. Thoreau found a rock he liked and placed it in his hut. A few days later he saw that it was gathering dust and took it back where he had found it, but I supposed I would have to live with the poster.

It started to seem like a good idea to stay in Eugene and live an interesting life. I could even ask May to come, though she probably wouldn't. On the other hand, I had a good job in Phoenix that I could probably get back. I talked about my dilemma with Yowie while we washed dishes.

"It's the best job I've ever had."
"You don't seem to like it much."   "True."
"Stay here, you'll develop more in line with your own nature."
"I'd have to resign."
"Send 'em a postcard."

That afternoon, I counted up my money and told Chan that I

organizing a commune in Eugene."

"What fun," she said. "I'm going back to school in Oakland a few weeks early to work on some projects. I can take you that far." For the next hour or so we talked about everything. It was a little after eight, rush hour in full tilt, when Carol dropped us on a downtown Oakland corner and after pointing out where we would stand to hitch across the bridge to San Francisco, drove away, both Kim and I watching until she turned and we could no longer see her. We continued watching for a second as though she might reappear.

"She's a brave lady," Kim finally said, "giving a ride to somebody as grouchy as you."

I reached into my shirt pocket and showed Kim the sheet of paper with her phone number written on it. He looked closely. "Let me see that," he said, reaching for it. I folded the paper quickly and put it into my wallet. "I'm going to call her, too, next time I'm in Oakland. But right now, I think we should check out what happened while we were away from Hippieopolis."

We landed a ride in only a few minutes with a former offensive guard at Sacramento State named Zack Patterson. He had turned on, tuned in, given up his football scholarship and was driving back from Death Valley, where he worked as an extra in Antonioni's <u>Zabriskie Point</u>. He was going into the city to close out his bank accounts and from there back to Sacramento and he invited us to drive with him as far as he went. By the time we reached Sacramento that evening, he had decided to go with us to visit the commune.

Two mornings later, when we parked in front of the commune, Zack and Kim had decided to drive to Seattle, sell Zack's car, and use the money to fly to Hawaii. We had breakfast inside then said farewells, Pip and I seeing them off. At that nascent moment, the commune, a up close and sped away."

"I must have blinked," I said. "That's when I missed it."

Five-thirty AM. Not light but not dark either. Except for the phantom VW that Kim believed he had seen, no more than half a dozen cars had passed since midnight. Now, a shiny Mustang convertible tooled up Highway One, its head lights still on, and as it approached it seemed to be slowing, veering toward us.

"That car is slowing for us," Kim said. "Or do you think it's a phantom, too?"

Not a phantom but a top-down red Mustang convertible that pulled to a stop beside the road in front of us, music from the console, black leather seats and, impossible to appreciate then, the driver.

I hurried to open the door and, stepping back, pulled the passenger seat forward and held it so that Kim would have to enter first. "I guess I'll sit in back," he said. "By myself." He tossed his sleeping bag onto the rear seat and climbed in.

It was the end of summer and not yet autumn, seasonless. The sun rose as we moved along, illuminating the rounded grassy knolls and riparian tree-lined waterways leading to the ocean-cut crags and cliffs at the water's edge. I turned to see if Kim were taking this all in. He sat with eyes closed, his head pushed against the back seat.

"He's beautiful," the driver said.

"Yeah, he is." Everybody thought so. I felt like Spencer Tracy in a Clark Gable movie. Next time I lunged over the edge, I would do it with someone ordinary-looking.

"Where are you two going?" she asked.

"Oregon for now. I'm on vacation. Kim has a few weeks before he goes back to college. We're going to visit some friends who are

"House in New Orleans," and then the concert was over. By then Kim and I had been separated from the group in the milk truck and walked together back toward the highway. "I've had enough of Los Angeles," he said.

"We've been here about two hours."

"That's enough. Let's go to Oregon."

"Why not?" It was time to get to Eugene, where all the prospective members of the commune were finding their way. If we arrived early enough we might still get a bedroom. We got a ride with a Navy Seal on leave who explained that he had broken up with his girlfriend at the concert. After telling us that, he drove in silence for a while. "If you get a cut in the tropics," he said, finally, "you leave it exposed so that flies can lay their eggs in there. The babies eat the decaying flesh and help heal the injury."

"You mean maggots?" Kim asked.

"Yeah. Maggots. Then, if your survival is in jeopardy you can eat the maggots."

"Neat," I said.

A few miles further along, he explained how to leap into the air and break a tree branch with one karate kick, then dropped us at Oxnard. We landed a ride to Santa Barbara with an avocado farmer, and at midnight found ourselves on a silent stretch of Highway One in the very center of town. After the first hour, we began to take turns, one of us standing beside the road, ready to hitch, while the other sprawled on the grass or walked here and there. Hours passed, and the sky began to lighten.

"How long has it been since we even saw a car?" I asked.

"That gray VW," Kim answered. "About a minute ago. It slowed down, remember? I thought they were going to stop. Then they saw you passenger side, which had been designed so that a milkman might step quickly down, was open. There was a folding door, but when I tried to close it, it wouldn't budge.

"The door is just for looks," the driver said. "I keep meaning to get it fixed but just don't get around to it." He reached toward the glass wind chime and
tapped it with a finger. "That tinkle means an angel is getting stoned," he said, and passed a smoldering joint our way.

I passed. I didn't like the lethargy marijuana created in me. I also had no problem accepting that Bill Clinton had smoked marijuana without inhaling in his youth. I think that would seem impossible only to someone who had never passed on a toke in his life, or her life either.

By good fortune, the milk wagon was headed to the Long Beach music festival, and with luck we would arrive in time to catch the last performers, Eric Burdon and the Animals. After a few moments, the milk truck topped out at forty-five, the front end shook without stop, rattling the wind chimes and tossing all of us passengers from side to side. Besides the driver there were now eight of us aboard: a pair of young lovers enthralled by their own magnificence, three teenage boys huddled together like Delta Force Commandos surrounded by enemy, and a man in a suit, the neighbor of the driver, who had hitched a ride to a Monday morning business meeting in Laguna Beach. There were no seats in the truck and after a few miles we were all sprawled on the floor except for the man in the suit.

It was nearly twilight when we parked in a dirt field a half mile from the concert and began walking toward the music. The sound of the amplified guitars at that distance, in the fading light, among strangers, hung suspended, a regret with no resolution, reminding me that it was Sunday. We heard part of "Hangman" and an extended version of and I thought about charging to the rescue, but instead I rolled over noisily to face toward the center of the room, a dungeon of sorts. I think we both had accepted the possibility of sexual overtures as the cost of housing ourselves for the night. We didn't expect the endless beseeching interrupted by Kim's repeated denials that woke me. In dim illumination from the street, the room was a labyrinth of shadow folding into shadow, giving the walls a suggestion of dampness that I don't otherwise remember. Beneath the bed the floor was misshapen by shadows, piles of books and clothing dropped wherever.

"Let's get out of here," Kim said. I looked at the clock. "Two-fifty. It's two-fifty."

"It's a good time for getting out of here," Kim answered, beginning to roll up his sleeping bag. "Let's go to Los Angeles."

On the highway south, we ran out of hitchhiker fluid and waited beneath a street lamp for the next car, and the next car after that, and then the sky began to lighten and a white milk truck rolled toward us, one headlight burning. It stopped a few feet in front of us. The crystalline music of wind chimes hanging from the rear view mirror and the sharp tang of marijuana smoke wafted toward us. "'Wafted' is the right word there," Kim said looking over my shoulder. "It suggests motion combined with passivity."

"Why are you talking like that?" I asked.

"What do you mean?"

"You sound more like me than you."

"You can revise it later."

There were already six people in the milk truck, counting the driver. For a while, Kim and I stood in front, holding onto a safety bar above the windshield. This offered a good view of the road but was uncomfortable and potentially hazardous. The doorway on the

James's Yarn

How I Became the Historic 7th or 8th Member of the Yellow Sub

We were walking back from Coit Tower, Kim and I, on our sight-seeing tour of flower-child Mecca, and on our way to Eugene, Oregon, where friends were organizing a commune. First, we wanted to check out the hippies. I looked the part, more or less, but Kim, a painter, fulfilled the last tittle of hippie couture: ragged Levi's, blue and white striped work shirt, engineer's cap, and a red bandana around his neck. He might have been mistaken for Paul Bunyan, Casey Jones, and Jesse James all at once.

"Since you're writing about it," Kim said, "put down that this may wind up being your most expensive vacation ever."

"How did you know that I was writing?" I asked.

"You always fiddle with your earlobes when you're thinking about writing," he said. He lifted the sleeping bag from his shoulder, tossed it into the middle of the street, and it began rolling, gaining speed, downhill, into and through the nearest intersection and midway through the next block, where it veered away from the center of the road, up onto the sidewalk, and came to rest in the doorway of a tailor shop.

"Did you write that in?" Kim asked.

"It's in," I said. "But we have to decide where we're going to sleep tonight... and I'm hungry. Do you have any money?"

"Couple of bucks."

"We have enough for minestrone and sourdough rolls at Big Mike's Pool Hall. Maybe we'll see Lawrence Ferlinghetti." We didn't see Ferlinghetti, but Kim talked with this guy seated at the counter beside us who said we could stay with him for a night or two.

When I woke that night I could hear Kim saying, "no, no...,"

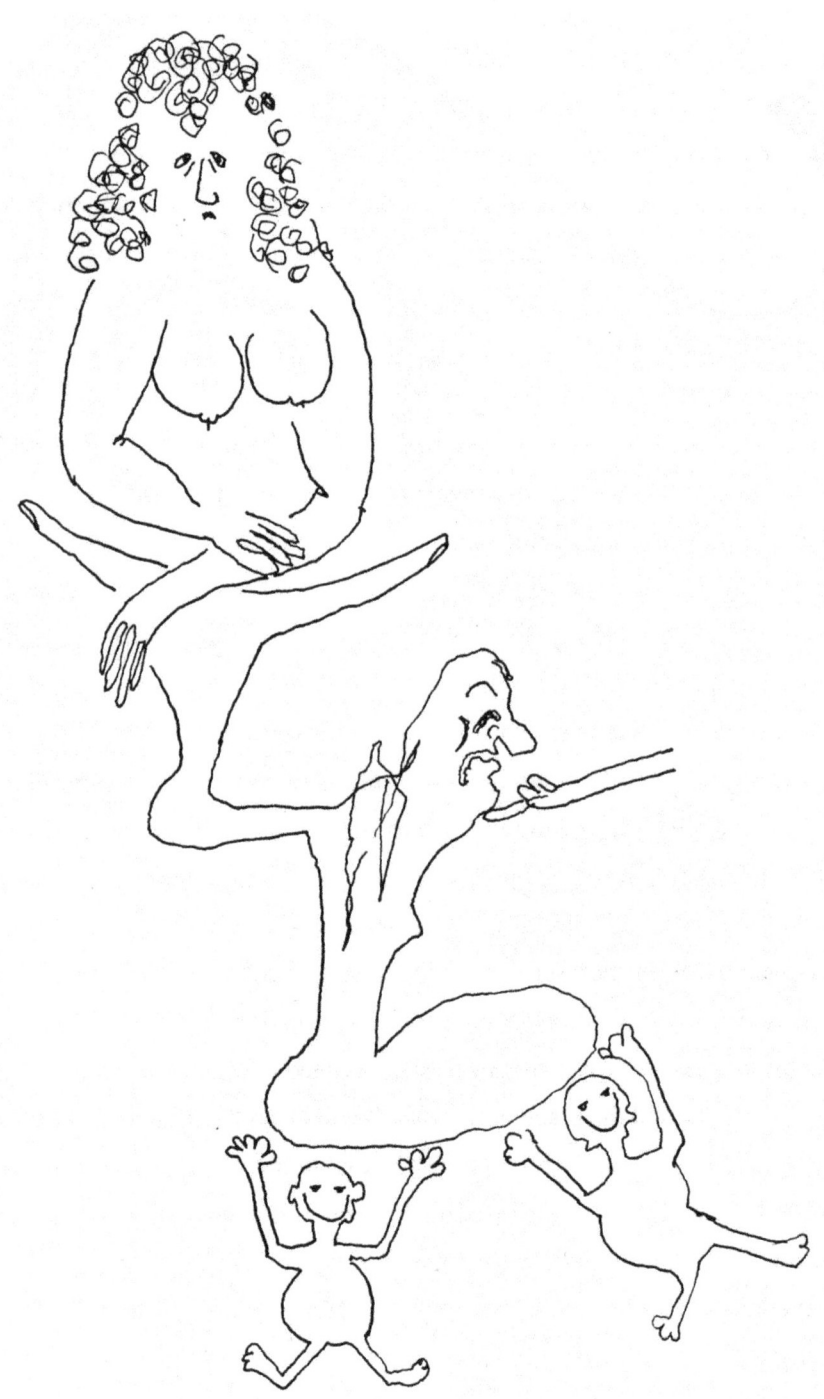

friends, Hatoon, and Mike Bakaty, and others. During the next few weeks we searched for a place to rent that seemed big enough and near enough to town, and had a rural feeling--and was cheap enough for us to afford.

It was beginning to feel unlikely to find a place meeting all our requirements when we found 2449 Floral Hill Drive: five bedrooms, two bathrooms, with a 'barn' down the hill, and lots of garden space. The cost? $150/mo. Remember, this was before the policies of the Reagan Administration added those zeroes to all the prices. The main house sat down from Floral Hill Drive and a parking space or two occupied the front if you approached from the town side. It was nerve-wracking exiting from this parking space since it meant backing up forcefully against a steep incline and out onto the road which may or may not have traffic. To the right of the house was a large stone patio retaining the hillside beyond which someone had constructed a flight of stairs leading to a small workshop space. We were later to use it as a bedroom. Pollo insulated it with wadded-up newspapers and cardboard stapled across the studs. Past this small one room (with windows) was a vehicle pullout leading back to the road, large enough for two or maybe three vehicles. All in all, it was ideal. I knew it to be right when I found an article from "Life" magazine on the 'acid-rock' groups of the day taped to the upstairs closet wall: There were the Doors in a closet with a TV; Cream sitting on a seemingly endless railroad track; the Mothers of Invention in a butcher shop; Jefferson Airplane on a child's plastic play structure. I later learned that a member of a local rock band had occupied the place before we did. The landlord, Jack De Santos, was very understanding and I felt him to be flexible if a few friends joined us later. Pollo cultivated a relationship with him, as did James Livingston when he came north from Phoenix. Very soon, the influx from the south would begin. As they say, "You had to be there to fully understand."

It didn't rain as much as 'they' said it did here; It was only an hour drive to the high Cascade Mountains, and an hour drive in the other direction to the vast Pacific Ocean; He had met some very interesting people here.

We looked around town and liked what we saw. Water, needless-to-say, was abundant. Then, with Pollo aboard, we drove to Seattle to stay with Quarrel and Doris Stockton and their new son, Luke. Another friend, Tom Cherrytree, was also staying with them temporarily. We had a huge spaghetti dinner, then drove around in Quarrel's re-painted bread van through the Ballard district and the University of Washington, where DeeDee taught, talking about the Black Panther's refusal to aspire to the prevailing "middle-class pathology." When it was time to head south, Tom decided to come to Phoenix with us. On the way, we dropped Pollo off at his house in Eugene. Back in Phoenix we began preparing ourselves to move to Eugene.

> **In the town where I was born**
> **Lived a man who sailed to sea**
> **And he told us of his life....**
> **Beatles**

Memory, as Goethe points out, is not static, but "eternally growing from the past."

Anita's family was more than a tad dismayed that we were moving so far away, and, for what? Nonetheless, in very little time, Tom Cherrytree, Anita, and I loaded up all our belongings and our new baby in the V-Dub and drove back to Eugene to stay with Pollo again. As we turned off the I-5 freeway and drove into Eugene on Franklin Blvd. Karisma was so amazed at what she saw that her jaw dropped open and her pacifier dropped out and rolled out through a hole in the floorboard. We never replaced it. Pollo was pursuing a graduate degree in fine art and in time we met a variety of his interesting

In April of '68, Karisma was born, and planning a move to the Pacific Northwest, I didn't renew my teaching contract. I bought a used VW Van (the vehicle of choice at the time) and early in June we headed out, brother Yowie, Malcolm and Mudra Simpson and I. Not knowing the necessity to downshift on the hills, I promptly burned the valves between Phoenix and Hell-A. We stayed at the house in L.A. of the parents of Sandra, Yowie's first wife, as a sort of emergency. They were not too pleased with the crowdies who arrived on their doorstep while the Van got its valves reground. Innocence has its shortcomings.

After leaving there, we tried to locate The Institute of Non-Violent Living on Joan Baez's property near Carmel. We failed and crashed by the roadside in sleeping bags. These were the days when you could do such a thing (even in California) and not raise anyone's ire. When we awoke the next morning (my 25th birthday) we heard on the radio that Robert Kennedy had been assassinated the previous night at a downtown hotel in Hell-A. A sinking feeling descended. Bobby Kennedy used to say, "We can do better."

We stayed in the war resistance house in East Palo Alto where they were making preparations to take a large flat bed truck with a band out on the road to educate folks about the immorality of the Vietnamese War. We drove to Sanford University and attended a demonstration with David Harris. Next we went to San Francisco, drove through the Haight-Ashbury District, and found a place to crash from a meeting held in the Glide Memorial Church near the panhandle of Golden Gate Park. I remember going to the park to smoke a joint. A couple of black guys came over to share a puff or two, and I noticed a button on one guy's shirt that said "Free Huey." When I asked who Huey was, they quickly moved off. Innocence has its benefits.

We persisted up the road to Eugene where we stayed with Pollo Smith and his son, Gagutz, friends from Tucson. Pollo told us that:
There was no 'out-of-state' tuition for graduate school at the Univ. of Oregon;

Chanren's Tale

HIGHJINKS AND VAGUE MISHAPS ABOARD THE YELLOW SUB

The entire science of wayfinding is based on dead reckoning. You only know where you are by knowing precisely where you have been and how you got to where you are.1

Community has been an important subtext of my life, but not something I paid particular notice of until recently. At ten or so, several friends and I built forts where we could hide out together. I suppose this is where my first awareness about community began. Much later, my wife Anita and I rented a small place in the Greek islands with my brother Yowell, and this experience helped to fore-ground the idea of intentional community.

In 1967, the year of "Sergeant Pepper's Lonely Hearts Club Band," Anita and I returned from a summer in Mazatlan, 'Nita to grad school, and me to another year teaching art at Manzanita Elementary, in Phoenix, Arizona. We had been talking and writing letters with our friends about a commune throughout the summer, and during that winter and early spring we began taking weekend sojourns into the Arizona countryside scouting out a suitable location for a "back to the land" communal living possibility, but the scarcity of water posed a problem wherever we looked.

Water, or the lack of it, is a major setback of living in Arizona. This lack has subtle effects. I remember an ASU art instructor in a class I took while Nita was doing course work in counseling. I brought in a portrait I'd done of Bob Dylan, in blue, with a fiery background. "There's no green in it," my instructor said. "How can you paint a picture with no green?" Of course, Arizona politics, that ghost machine of abstraction and laminated thinking shows a similar lack.

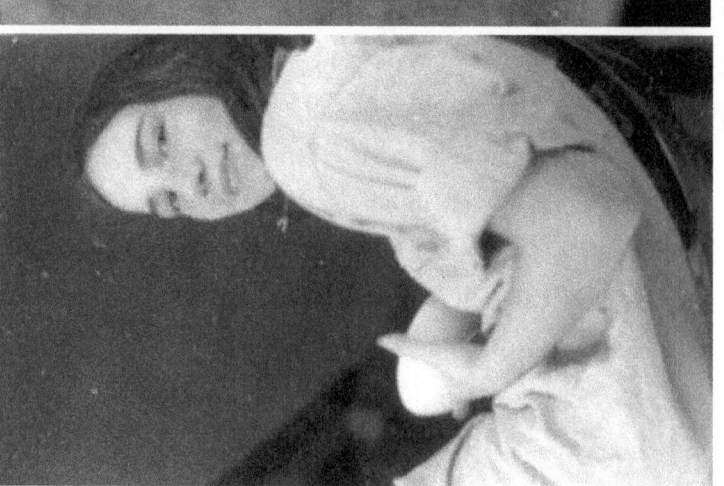

Candy and Katy

From l. Jerry, Anita and Chanren. "Whatcha doin, Jerry?"

Jerry's Account

Granola. That's right, granola. That's what I immediately recall when I look back forty-plus years in marvelous awe and high love at the Yellow Submariners, that quirky hip band of artists, artisans, musicians, herbalists, and Rolling-Stones-loving longhairs from Arizona who came to Eugene in the late 60s.

I was privileged to work and play and live and love with them, becoming an honorary Submariner. I was tremendously inspired to see them turn into a worker's collective, once a week, making granola for sale to pay the rent. I was mindful of their early example when I helped found the Hoedads, the forest-worker collective.

Making Granola. Good thing to do in a time of relentless blow-their-minds consciousness, while experiencing psychedelics, like peyote and psilocibin. Yah, you could feel the time's a changin'. Granola helped keep it grounded.

Looking back

Years later I began to see that my initial cry for companionship – as neighbors who saw one another almost daily – had, partly for economic reasons, crowded us into a single house. What we were then striving for was to interrelate as family, but some were people who barely knew one another. Several of us had been friends for 10 years (some now going on 50), but few had lived together as family. There were exceptions, brothers Yowie and Chanren, and Chanren and Anita, and me and Doris, plus another couple or two. Yet, all but one of the marriages split under the stresses and temptations of the Sub lifestyle. The naïvely idealistic goal of living in harmony in such crowded and interdependent conditions when we had so little history of close relationships was too much to expect.

The Sub experience was extraordinary and was productive of imagination and relations. But it was also destructive, painful, stressful. It nourished a few relationships and destroyed many others. I am thankful that my long friendships with Yowie, Pollo, and Chanren were nourished and survive still. However, many of the painful and destructive events of the Sub days are ignored by those of us who have chosen to write of our times there.

Now, at age 74 and most of the desperado gone out of me, I have two children besides Luke, whom I have not seen for over 20 years. Both the later children have graduated college and live nearby. Alice, my wife of 34 years, is recently retired and we are comfortable in our unmortgaged home.

next fall season, I and several others were taken on as new members. I planted on several jobs over the winter and spring and apparently Jerry and the original members felt the expansion was a success as the next fall they opened the coop further to new membership.

Inexperienced people signed up in droves to do this very tough work. Having briefly returned to stay at the Sub in its terminal days, I recruited Submariners Elvis, and Jay and Mud Button, plus street friends Jack and Gary and a couple others. Head Hoedaddys Rust and Ed Wimple decided the new Hoedads should be organized into a number of sub-crews that worked independently on jobs. My recruits and I named our crew "The J-Roots." The name caused a scandal. What was intended as humor was not funny to the founding fathers. The reason our joke got no sympathy was the fact that a "j-root" was the result of a failed attempt to plant a tree deeply enough. The curled root would cause the tree to die. When discovered by the USFS inspectors, who actually dug up many randomly-selected trees, j-roots and other mistakes caused the group's pay for the whole job to be docked. Nevertheless, in the great confusion and chaos of the Hoedad expansion, during which around 300 people came and went, planted for a very short time, some only hours, and quit, the J-Roots soldiered on, mostly being assigned to other crews to help train incoming new members.

Soon after landing at the Sub I began taking welding classes at Lane Community College under a federal grant for people on welfare. I guess I had not yet fully renounced the economic ratrace. For over a year I half-heartedly attempted to learn high tech welding on the belief it would lead to a good job that did not involve much in the way of abstract thinking. This hope was inspired by the descriptions of the course that enticed me and two dozen or so young fellows to enroll. After the year and a half I learned there were no decent jobs for welders in the Eugene area. For that matter, there had been a growing oversupply of welders in the whole state due to the training programs at LCC and elsewhere that had been running for several years. The "good jobs" for which they were training us were in Alaska, on the transcontinental pipeline. I had no interest in moving to Alaska so this was a major disappointment and I quit the class. This was about the time Doris and I moved out of the Sub in our attempt to reconcile differences that were threatening to end our marriage.

Not so young and truly confused during three wild years after leaving the Sub in 1972 — and abandoning Doris and our son Luke— I traveled the country, living on the street, in my pickup truck, in my tipi in the Kalmiopsis Wilderness in Southern Oregon. For a couple of years I was a "hippy" — even though I was a bit old (then 35) for the part and struggling to leave adolescence behind.

Treeplanting

For several years after leaving the commune I worked during late fall, winter, and early spring in the national forests planting conifer trees. At the time, 1972, the Hoedads were an established coop of about twelve planters who contracted work from the US Forest Service and BLM. I knew one of the leaders of the Hoedads, Jerry Ferrox, from his visits to the Sub and I played on his social conscience to let me join the coop. The our lives as I wandered about the place. The kitchen and all the implements and serving bowls were meager, pathetic tools that allowed us to sustain our grip on existence. I felt these experiences as harrowing ordeals having to do with death and grief. Yet I repeated them again and again. I really can't say why.

To make financial ends meet in the Sub quite a number of folks invented a granola-cereal and set about manufacturing it in the kitchen. It was quite a success after initial trials. The details are no doubt best described by others who actually did the work. Also, Doris and I and Luke obtained a welfare grant. In those days the accounting for where that money went was a bit lax, and so it was no violation to use it to pay the communal rent. The grant raised about $150 a month and on one or more occasions was most of the Sub's monthly income.

Among my miscellaneous memories, I recall a multi-vehicle trip several of us took into the coast range—near Veneta, I think—looking for a rural site to get back to the land. I was real excited and wildly struck out to traverse the perimeter, charging through the brush. I eventually made it to the woods, but only a couple years later and not in the company of my old friends and communards.

Somehow, the land-line telephone (pre cell-phones) at the Sub was in mine and Doris' name. When the US Congress passed a special tax on all long distance calls, the money to go directly to fund the war in Vietnam, there was a political protest. Naturally we Submariners all agreed to withhold the money for the long distance from our payments. After a few months Agent Jones from the US IRS came and towed the van away in lieu of the taxes. While they were hooking up the tow truck I rushed into the house and got Yowie to sign & post-date the van title as the current owner. I thought this would stop them, but Jones just laughed and told the driver to take it away equipment as I could gather. I hung stuff on the walls on nails and had people sign a checkout list. Since I wasn't about to sit out in the tool room and wait for customers; signing out tools was to be on the honor system. That is about all that needs to be said—except that the fate of the tool room could have been prophetic regarding the naive idealism at the heart of the Sub itself.

A second effort at finding a role was to temporarily take on the job as custodian of the marijuana stash. Gina and Double T, old friends of Yowie, had arrived from Tucson bringing their homegrown weed, almost seven pounds they said, including seeds and large stems. My only qualification for the position, as none of us had ever seen so much contraband in one place, was my having been busted in L.A. in 1965 for giving two joints to a young undercover cop. After 30 days in the L.A. County felony dungeon I made bail. Several months later I was given a sentence of three years probation.

Soon after landing at the Sub I dropped some acid. It was I think my second trip, the previous having been years before. This time my drug trip included a sexual adventure with one of the unattached women. I remember the trip well because this was my first extra-marital sexual adventure in three years. During the trip and the sex I renounced entirely the guilt and remorse I had felt deeply for years for being sexually unfaithful in my relationship with Doris. At the time I had the overwhelming certainty that I, as a male human, was not meant to be monogamous, that it was against my animal nature, my masculine identity. I resolved never again would I submit to the guilt and the sexual restrictions of the past several years!

I went on to drop acid and other psychedelic drugs with some regularity for the months I stayed at the commune. I can only recall a half dozen or so of these "trips" that I remember as pleasant. Yet I did it again and again. My most memorable trips were perceptions of the pathos of meal, toilets, snores, etc. Be careful what you wish for.

This Yellow Submarine was a medium-sized yellow house, semi-submerged below the level of a narrow, pot-holed street in a residential neighborhood. When it eventually held over 20 full-time residents, the social dynamic truly resembled a submarine. I was irrevocably committed to joining the group sooner or later.

Partly the decision was based on what I'd recently learned about the so-called "Counter Culture," the "tune in, turn on, and drop out" culture. Moving to the hippy commune for me meant dropping out of the ratrace of the American Dream. I was giving up on the academic career that had never fit particularly well. I was getting off the capitalist economic ladder. A future of wage slavery had become an intolerable burden, insulting to my free spirit.

Life In The Yellow Submarine Commune

In late-July, 1969, Doris and I and our infant son Luke finally arrived at the Sub to live. The group, then numbering about 9, had already been living together for a year or so. Some roles were established, otherwise various struggles were underway. As the next to oldest male (Wayne at 60 not being active in the pecking order rivalry), I semiconsciously felt I needed a role, somewhat as a leader I suppose. (This account is, of course, reflective and my motives and this perspective only became clear to me many years later. At the time I was just thrashing around in the dark.)

My struggle for a role was definitely a chaos-producing factor. I made up roles, tool custodian, dope guard, etc., and had a real verbal screamer with Pollo over how to dig a sewer ditch - even though I knew next to nothing about the job. The tool custodian thing lasted only a few weeks. After some complaints in meetings about tools being lost, I made a room in the barn into a storage place for as many of the Sub's tools and

Quarrel's Complaint

Quarrel Writes to Get Friends Together Again

In 1967 I was 29 years old, a grad student in philosophy at the University of Illinois at Champaigne-Urbana. I lived in a student room there and hitchhiked semi-weekly to Macomb where Doris, my wife of three years, was an instructor at the small college, Western Illinois University

I was homesick for my hometown and wrote my homies, Pollo and Yowie, that there was nothing I valued in the world more than their companionship. I said that more than anything I wanted to return to the camaraderie of our idyllic student days around the University of Arizona campus where, just a year earlier, we'd hung out and shared experiences regularly. I guess it was somewhat of a love letter—and maybe it helped to inspire Yowie and Pollo and Chanren to gather in Eugene.

I passed up an offer of a teaching fellowship at the Champaigne-Urbana Campus and went with Doris to Seattle where she had obtained a fellowship at the University of Washington. Some months after landing in Seattle there came word that Pollo had visited Eugene and others were planning to follow and settle. I decided to give up on the business of academic philosophy and to move to Eugene and live with my old friends in the Yellow Submarine - whatever that was.

Months later we visited the "commune" and I got quite a shock: what I had wished for had come true but I didn't recognize it. This chaotic social scene was exciting and somewhat threatening, partly because the reality was so different from my imagination. Except for casual reading about the Haight-Ashbury scene, I'd not known there were such things as "hippy communes"! My original impulse I'd written about back in Illinois was to return to the days of bliss we'd enjoyed as students in Tucson, at the U of A – but not all crammed into a single house, sharing nearly every

Until I developed some degree of empathy and communal spirit, I did not fare that well in our commune. My concept of minimal expense in order to have the free time to pursue my art did not happen. I did no sculptures while I was at the commune. I dropped out of the MFA program at the university.

I returned from Mexico to live back in Tucson. I scraped by with various less than full time jobs. I made sandals. I taught ceramics classes. I had drafting jobs. I got word from Chanren that Sadie had died of brain cancer.

Eventually I got a full time job with the local school district as a maintenance worker. I retired with 18.89 years of credited service.

I met my wife on a train leaving Paris. We have been married 33 years. We have three grown children. Looking back on my life, the continuous thread seems to be putting effort into learning to get along with people.

decided by consensus. Chanren was frustrated when I brought home a puppy. It had been unavoidable. I was walking down a street and a very pretty woman in a Navy peacoat was walking toward me, and looking me right in the eye, and smiling. When we were face to face she opened the top of the peacoat, revealing a tiny brown puppy, and said "would you like a puppy?" This was the first time I was aware of how easily men can be manipulated by women. But I digress. There had been no consensus. Another time I built a large table for the living room. Once again this had been done without a consensus.

When the commune started, I was in graduate school at the U. and was working for an architectural firm. Gagutz was at a day care center during the day. After I was laid off, and dropped out of graduate school, I did participate more in commune life. This also was when I started my relationship with Dana.

No one that I know that was in the commune has ever put themselves in another group environment except Chanren and Lindy. They lived for a while at a Buddhist community, The Land of a Thousand Buddhas. Looking back, there were some great times had by all. But there was a fair share of pain and heartache. The commune went on another year after we left. As described to me, the situation grew darker. It seems that I heard mention of heroin, and other bad scenes, but I am not sure.

With all the current economic uncertainty, the need for individuals to group together for the common good may have a compelling urgency. A society of nuclear families, all ensconced in their separate homes, may be a luxury that many can no longer afford. The first steps have been modest. Families that have lost their homes have moved in with relatives. Sons and daughters that cannot find employment have moved back in with their parents. There are many contemporary tribal cultures, but our tribal past is quite distant. What might be the glue that holds together individuals who may have no practice with sharing, compromise, and the like?

my parents. I was sitting in a plaza in Matzatlan looking at a yellow cathedral, and it felt as though a bucket of sorrow, thick as molasses, was poured over me. I returned to Tucson, reunited with Dana and Gagutz, and Dana and I lived together for over a year. Gagutz and I then led a somewhat bachelor existence in what had been a Chinese market.

I met Dana again many, many years later, and we talked a bit. It is surprising to learn something about a person that had been missed before. I hadn't realized how important family was to her, and how much she was a woman who could set her mind to a goal, and be totally committed to it. Her husband is a successful artist, not an easy task to accomplish. My thought was that this was partly due to her support of him in achieving what he had set out to do. Dana was very pretty and had a beautiful voice, which might have obscured my ability to see her deeper qualities. I did always think that her personality was one that made being with her pleasant and smooth, even when we were no longer a couple. However, Dana thought that we fought all the time. Once, back in our Hippy days, we went to the local astrologer at the Hippy cafe in downtown Eugene to get our charts done. She said we would always be friends. She said nothing relating to our romantic future. I wondered about it at the time. The tact of silence.

Life Goes On

I am now an old man, and have suffered the slings and arrows of outrageous fortune, and the vagaries of fate, and all that. I look back on the commune experience. It really was a once-in-a-lifetime sort of thing. What to make of it? What other hackneyed phrase to throw out while waiting for some coherent thoughts? It was the best of times, it was the worst of times? While my motivation for joining the commune had been economic, Chanren and his brother Yowie had definite ideas about how we should live. All property should be held in common, and all decisions involving commune life should be fumes into the interior of the van where we were trying to sleep and may have distorted my perception. Looking out the window as we were coming into the bay area, the snaking freeway ramps and roads had a Dante's inferno aspect in the nighttime glare of the big overhanging road lights.

Grigsby lived in a comfortable home in one of the suburbs, and we settled in, and the weekend stretched out to almost a week before we decided it was time to return to Oregon. There was an onramp in Berkeley that was said to be the perfect place to hitch a ride north. Dana and I were picked up quickly and made an uneventful trip back.

I don't know how many people were unhappy with me this time, but certainly Pam was. Did I experience remorse at the time, or was I merely sheepish? Empathy was not my strong suit.

Life went on. I was to visit a final indignity on Pam. It was a dark and stormy night. Smokey and his wife, Doris, and Dana and I were listening to music up in the attic, which had previously been my bedroom. (One of the adjustments to commune life was to give up the attic and move my bed into what had been my sandal workshop, the playhouse near the main house.) There were intertwining histories between all of us and I was very uncomfortable. I called Pam and told her I was feeling very uncomfortable and could she come over. She got a neighbor to give her a ride on his motorcycle and arrived wet from the rain. She had broken her glasses getting off the motorcycle. So there I was, sitting on the attic floor with one arm around Dana and the other around Pam. I did not feel more comfortable and neither did she, and she left shortly thereafter.

Was it the rain and the gray skies day after day? Whatever the reason, weeks later, Dana, Gagutz, and I left the commune for the sunny southland. The roughly conceived plan was to travel to Mexico to buy craft goods and then return to Oregon to sell them. By the time we arrived in Flagstaff, Dana and I had decided to part company. I traveled to Mexico alone and left Gagutz with down the street, there was no sense of perspective. It was as though I was looking at a flat painting. I also noticed that people driving by all looked like werewolves.

We decided to drive to Hendricks Park to watch the sunset. The others tried to convince me to let one of them drive but I drove to the park. We stood at the edge of a hill and watched the sun go down. Spectacular!

Driving back in the dark, everything seemed reduced to tiny colored dots. Physicists say that what we normally see as solid is mostly empty space, so I thought, "Wow, so this is what reality is like."

The next morning I woke up and had acquired a periodic peculiar laugh. I couldn't control it and decided it would be best not to go to work for a few days. I can now describe it as the sort of laugh one could hear on the Bevis and Butthead show. When Mike and Janet went back to California, their antique wood-burning cook stove, blue and white, was hauled over to the commune.

A Trip to San Francisco

We all have regrets, but one that stands out in my memory is the trip Dana and I took to San Francisco. One of the commune visitors was a young woman named Pam. She was a kind spirited, gentle person. She appeared to have an interest in me. However, I treated her quite casually. Pam liked my son, Gagutz, and one day offered to take him with her for the weekend.

What had happened the previous week was that a friend from San Francisco, Grigsby, had come up for a visit. He found the commune much to his liking, but after a few days he was ready to return to San Francisco.

With Gagutz away for the weekend, a free ride to San Francisco, spending time alone with Dana away from the commune—the pieces seemed to fit together so nicely.

And so we were off to San Francisco. Grigsby's old hippy van leaked exhaust

Sex was what seemed most important to me. Not that I was always in bed with someone, but I was always thinking about how I wished that I were in bed with someone. It was easy to meet women at the University, and I had relationships with several. The relationships would only last a month or two. I suppose there are a variety of reasons someone might want to have sex. For me, it was quite a bit about being seen as likeable, and being accepted by another person. Since a woman literally opens herself up to a man, that assumption could be made. Imagine the missionary position. Assumptions, however, are suspect.

A Visit to the Daily Flash

I met a couple from Berkeley, Mike and Janet. They had rented an abandoned neighborhood store in the middle of town. They decided to start a head shop, selling pipes, candles, and other hippie items. The sign over the door said "The Daily Flash". I visited the store often and got to know them.

The front area was the shop space, and they lived in the back. There was also a basement, which was appointed with pillows, and music was piped into the ductwork in the ceiling.

A friend of mine, Patrick, came up to visit from San Francisco. We decided to visit the Daily Flash. However we were acting, it managed to get on Mike's nerves. He offered me coffee and we went to the basement to listen to the Rolling Stones. Little by little, the music sounded stranger and stranger. At some point I asked Mike what he had put in the coffee. He said, "Oh, just a bit of Blue Cheer. You needed it." I was upset about being drugged and he offered to give me some Thorazine, which he said would bring me down.

I found the state I was in to be interesting so I declined. I kept saying, "It's not my fault. I'm not in control, and I am responsible for raising a small child." I walked around the streets for a little while. I was fascinated—looking

Harsh and angry would describe my reaction to Gagutz's deviations from the straight and narrow. There were only a few children in the commune, and I had noticed him receiving many small lectures about what to do and not do, but I was oblivious to how I was being observed by others when I gave him an angry spanking. My treatment of Gagutz has been something I have greatly regretted. I now have other sons, and my treatment of them has been altered as far as physical punishment is concerned. Much of the credit must be given to my wife, who is firmly committed to parenting without corporal punishment and the like. Additionally, over the years, the level of anger and frustration with life has lessened, and I just can't build up a head of steam to go around hitting children.

Sex, Drugs, and Rock and Roll

I was curious about the drugs that were available, but never was terribly interested in them.

I liked the music of the period, but did not have a passion for it. However, music was part of what made the commune time special. The record player was in the kitchen and sometimes I would get to listen to the same record over and over and over whether I wanted to or not.

There was a festival of sorts one time at Skinner's Butte Park. I don't know who was playing but we were all dancing around on the grass. Also, there was a really good local band that played at a bar near campus. Country Joe and the Fish played a concert at a peculiarly shaped building at the county fair grounds. The Grateful Dead were friends with Ken Kesey. They came up and gave a free concert at the ballroom at the university. I was spending time with Dana at that time. We went to that concert together. I had a shirt with big puffy sleeves and I had long hair. Her dress was loose. All our clothing was flopping around as we danced. It was a great night.

India, and one thing led to another, and he woke up in a facility in the U.S. He had met Sadie or her roommate and would come over and go to sleep in front of the fireplace. One day, he had, perhaps, a chemically enhanced revelation that Sadie was the one for him. What followed was that she ended up spending a couple of weeks with him, then deciding to be with me, and then deciding to go back with him. This went on through a number of cycles.

One day, Sadie and I were at the commune. Ferrox came rolling up on his Honda 50 motor scooter. He was a pretty big guy, so seeing him on the small scooter had a comical aspect. In the commune, it wasn't as though you could lock the door and keep people out. He came in and said he had come for Sadie. The only thing I thought to do was to grab him. We fell to the floor and rolled around. What was peculiar was that we weren't wailing away at each other. It had an aspect of ritualized combat. Quite soon, several people came and separated us. He told Sadie to come with him and she did. They both got on the tiny scooter and putted away. It was late afternoon and they were literally riding off into the setting sun. I went up to the attic and cried and cried, which pretty much purged me of the sadness I had anticipated going on and on.

Also, my punishment of Gagutz should be noted. Gagutz was not a holy terror, not even mischievous. He didn't always do exactly as the adults might have liked, but his infractions were minor except for the time he and Jeffrey, May and James' son, started a fire in the "barn". Luckily, it was noticed and put out in time.

Not every commune member was active in the resistance, which had non-violence as a core value, but the feeling of non-violent behavior was pervasive. I came from a working class background, with corporal punishment taken for granted. Two of my mother's brothers left home at 16. My grandfather would tie them to the bed and beat them. I remember being led to the basement by my mother, one hand holding mine, and the other holding a cherry switch. It seemed like divine intervention when lightning struck the cherry tree.

to try commune life. Shortly after arriving, these marriages began to unravel. There were quite a few single people either living in the commune or visiting. This was an era of sexual experimentation, and there could have been a sign over the front door, "Let the experiment begin." My vivid image at an encounter group was of one of the group whose marriage had disintegrated. He was very sad, and he was crying. His head was down and there was a drop hanging from his nose that he did not brush away. I stared, wondering if it was a tear that had worked its way down, or if it was from his nose.

The Wrestling Match

During the time I was at the commune, it was perhaps surprising but encouraging that there was no physical violence over the various stresses and conflicts that arose with a group of individuals packed together. Well, not exactly never. There was a couple who were active in the Resistance movement. Their relationship survived their commune experience. Some called them the Lilliputians. Neither of them was at all violent toward anyone else in the commune, but they would have quite physical confrontations with each other. Their room was next to the kitchen. The kitchen was a gathering place so people were often there. They would close the door, but anyone in the kitchen could hear that unsettling sound of flesh being struck—over and over again. While no one directly observed, the sense was that it was about an equal give and take.

Another instance of things getting physical was the encounter I had with a frequent visitor, Ferrox. I had met a young woman, Sadie, and would go spend time with her as often as possible. I was in love. One complaint about me was that I would leave Gagats at the commune, and the commune women would feel obligated to care for him at some level, without having agreed to it. She had an apartment near campus. It had a fireplace. As told to me, Ferrox had wandered into Eugene by way of India. He had been in the Peace Corps in of residents, the Buttons, and the relative was looking for Lindy or Geary. These guys had been drinking and dropping pills. One of the trio was talking to my son, Gagutz, and he was telling them what life was like at the commune. He became greatly offended by the thought of a little boy being raised in the commune environment. He got out his knife and said he was going to cut me up. The other two got into the act of berating me. There was little I could do so I let them rant and rave. Eventually, they started arguing among themselves. I didn't get cut up but some posters were slashed with the knife that was meant for me. Talk calmed down. The relative mentioned that he was on parole for something. Somewhere along the line, word had gotten out to a neighbor and a policeman showed up. I told the policeman everything was all right, figuring that this little melodrama would violate one guy's parole and he would be off to jail. I got thanked for that and they went on their way.

The Encounter Group

Wayne had a girlfriend, June, who was connected with a conscious raising group, the Senoi Institute, which organized and led encounter groups. These would go on for 24 hours, and address individual and group problems.

The first one was given at a motel on the coast, Gull Haven. There were a number of people who were not happy with my actions, so I was called on the carpet. This went on for some time but I don't remember it as being particularly traumatic. Maybe I liked the attention. Months later, life in the commune did get upsetting for me. Some people wanted me to leave. Terry, later Terra, told me straight out that she and others did not want me to live there anymore. I had signed the lease for the house and decided to just hunker down. Eventually, the people who wanted me to leave were gone and I had also modified my behavior.

There were more encounter groups. I have only one vivid image from all the groups. There had been a number of married couples that had decided commune. After she arrived, she spent the first day crying. But within a short period of time she was baking bread for everyone. Gagutz, Mom, and I had a great time one day. We drove over to the dunes park outside Florence. It was a beautiful day and she enjoyed herself.

A Trip to the Coast

Trips to the dunes park would occur from time to time. This time everyone was going. I had met a young woman from the L.A. area at school and she came with me.

When the group had set up camp, she and I wandered off. We ended up in a sort of mini-cave in a depression in the dunes. We didn't seem to have much to say to each other. She was pretty. I also noticed that she had crusty eyelashes. One might imagine what happened next, but I could not generate any interest in her. We started back to camp. We encountered a family at a campsite, and my son, Gagutz, was with them. The father gave me a stern lecture. He said that Gagutz had got lost while we hippies were off screwing, and that it wasn't right. I just let him rail, and then we went on our way. The commune women were beginning to prepare for a meal. I decided I wanted to go swimming, so I left to find a pool in the dunes. When I got back, the women were upset. The man who had lectured me had worked himself up to boiling point, and had headed over to our camp to beat me up. Since I was not there, he yelled at the women and then left.

A Disreputable Trio Invades the Commune

Everyone was packing up for another trip to the dunes. It was such a perfect sunny day that I decided to stay at the commune and have a peaceful quiet day. But life can be unpredictable. Not long after everyone left, there was a knock on the door. There were three rather rough and ready looking guys standing, who invited themselves in. One was a relative of a later wave

Mono Strikes

Only a few weeks into the start of the commune, I came down with mononucleosis. My bed was in the attic. The bathroom was down a flight of stairs and it was all I could do to make it down and back. I had no energy at all. The women in the commune brought my meals up to me. I think there had been a compromise. They agreed to bring up the food, but emptying bedpans was not going to happen.

This went on for weeks. Life was quite boring. Some people thought there was "action" in the attic, but there was no energy for that. I had laid claim to the attic when we first rented the house. It was a long skinny space that stretched across the length of the main house. I had picked that area since it had the most privacy. There was no cross traffic through it. However, that privacy somewhat separated me from the communal feeling. There was quite a bit of sexual experimentation going on downstairs. I did not have the best attitude which might partly explain why, until close to the end of my stay, I had only a couple of brief encounters of that sort with any of the women in the commune.

Mother Visits

I had written my parents about my illness, and my mother came up to Oregon to visit me. It didn't occur to me that this visit was at all unusual. My mother would not have been described as outwardly affectionate. She had been a teacher for years before getting married. Keeping thirty-five restless children under control may have set the tone for the way she parented. Her first child died shortly after being born. I was born a year or two after that. I was sickly and her mother told her that I would not survive to adulthood. That a sixty-year-old woman would jump on a bus to go take care of her son had to be an expression of mother love. She had no sense of what life was like in the

Pollo's Picaresque Exploits

Preface

I was living in Pennsylvania. My marriage had ended and I was raising my son as a single parent. I got fired from my drafting job. I was in contact with my college sculpture teacher.

My teacher suggested that I enter graduate school at the University of Oregon. At the time, there were no out of state tuition fees for graduate school.

I arrived in the Eugene, Oregon area on Christmas Eve, and slept in my car at a rest area. I met people quickly and had places to stay until I found a tiny house to rent in an alley.

Friends from Arizona suggested that we start a commune.

People arrived; Chanren, who was a friend of a friend, and others, and a search was on for a place to rent.

What pushes a person along in life? Some people have strong beliefs, or strong commitments to a cause, or connection to family or a group.

My tiny house was going to be torn down soon to make way for apartments. I had aspirations of becoming an artist. Sharing expenses with a group of people would allow me more time to pursue my art.

I had much to learn about living in a group.

It was sunny when we moved in, so it must have been in summer or early fall. Yowie, Chanren, and I had an argument in the kitchen, early on. I have no idea what the argument was about, but I was screaming. Looking at their faces, it seemed that this extreme expression was not something they were used to. I never saw them yell or scream. Much time has passed. The memories are of incidents, ones that were dramatic enough to resist being covered over by what followed.

and a close friend who applied with me.
Part-time student, part-time employee at the University of Oregon.
Family far away on the East Coast.
Interviewed and accepted!

Where were we?
Above a beautiful rhododendron park
on the edge of Eugene, Oregon, USA.
A plain house on the corner of a road becoming rural,
a one-block street overlooking a sloping field in the back.
How many bedrooms?
The back porch was my sleeping space with stars, fresh air,
a mat on the floor with an Indian print bedspread.

What was it like?
Cooking and eating together; meetings;
sharing drugs, parties, possessions and money.
Experiencing a friend's nightmare drug experience of bugs crawling over her.
Making "Harmony Grits" cereal for selling.
Waking in the middle of the night to find a friend, on drugs, staring at me.
Wandering on drugs in the park.
The woman who "flashed," i.e., no underwear, or so it was said.
Dancing on the roof of a car at an outside party;
rock music, the Beatles, the Doors, Janis.
My cat hit by a car on the road and buried by another commune friend, wondering if she was truly dead.
Artwork by friends.
Gardening.
Neighbors.
Friends.

Guided by the Southern Cross

Gale's Story

Why did we come together?
Out of the "normalcy" of the fifties,
Commie-baiting, McCarthy, economic stability, suburbs?
Into the sixties—Vietnam War, hallucinogens, flower children,
the civil rights struggles.
National/global expressions
of youthful experimentation and anti-war politics.
An ideology of community, sharing, and loving
from the heritage of older communities--Oneida, Amish, and others.
Politics of resistance to war waged by the US in SE Asia,
peace-mongering. Seeking spiritual renewal and transcendence:
yoga, meditation, hallucinogenic mind-altering drugs,
Timothy Leary and Ram Dass.
Openness—sexual and relationship possibilities, encounter groups.

Who were we?
White, middle-class, mostly in our twenties,
Some former college students.
One child, one baby, several teens in and out,
an older couple who visited. Men and women, shifting pairs.
Long hair on men and women, beards on the men,
hair under the arms and on the legs of the women.
Flowing colorful clothing or work clothes.

How did I get there?
Post-divorce, friends who were involved,

Contents

Guided by the Southern Cross

Gale's Story	1
Pollo's Picaresque Exploits	3
Quarrel's Complaints	16
Jerry's Account	23
Chanren's Tale: *Hijinks* and *Vague Mishaps Aboard the Yellow Sub*	26
James's Yarn: *How I Became the Seventh or Eighth Member of the Yellow Submarine*	31
Yowie's Interviews With Jay and Candy Button, 9/28/11, Geary Button the following day	55
Footnote Sources	96

Mariners' Prologue

This book is about a commune--a group of people in an open-ended living arrangement between the years 1968-71. Thirteen individuals from those years have submitted accounts. Several former members declined to contribute, and others are deceased, or could not be found. We dedicate our efforts to those crewmembers we know have passed on: Wayne Amos, Tom Emmens, Phil Borgias, and Tom Cherrytree.

These introductory remarks are co-authored. The rest of the text is a collection of accounts by individual authors, as noted.

Unsolicited Commentary
Regarding the Subvoyage of the Yellowmarine

"Adrenaline encounters tear gas" Razzamatazz Tribune

"Indigenous mythology tagged on the dark arts of corporatocracy"
               The Modju Gazette

"Sorcerer's rock prosody" Merchandisers' Globe

"Kava and Ashwaganda in their chem-trails…" Yi-Ha Roshi

"The reignbeau's heavenarches, the fairy ferse time, where the hand of man has never set foot, best intentions, cutthroat ties, once current puns, quashes quotatoes, crocodile tears, kisses from the antipodes, deoxidized carbons, blackeye lenses, fluefoul smut, alphybetty formed verbiage, ahems and ahahs, stinksome inkenstink"
               Rhoda Dandrums

"…the last generation of printed books on the planet and <u>this</u> is what we get?!?"

               Prof. A. Runcible Spoon
               Chair of the Dept. of Psychopodiatry,
               Sofa of Mythopoeia, Universalty of Atlantis

"You know, the novelty's wearing real thin. I've already got a damn crick in my neck trying to read this crap upside-down!"

               Saxby Strutmince
               Lead Economist in the Investment Bank
               Slash Legal House of Pilfer, Rapine & Plunder

Voyage of the Yellow Submarine

A multi-voice chronicle of life in a commune

By
Tuna Cole, Pip Cole, and Crew

Crew members in this collective narrative include Nepal T Blalock; Joe, Tammy, and Gary Brittain; Vernette Christensen; James Livingston; John Richey; Jerry Rust; Gail Sanford; Pollo Smith; and Quarrel Stockton—in addition to Tuna and Pip Cole.

www.ingramcontent.com/pod-product-compliance
Lightning Source LLC
Chambersburg PA
CBHW022119080426